Colorado's Historic Schools

Linda Wommack

TWODOT®

ESSEX, CONNECTICUT
HELENA, MONTANA

A · TWODOT® · BOOK
An imprint of Globe Pequot, the trade division of
The Rowman & Littlefield Publishing Group, Inc.
4501 Forbes Blvd., Ste. 200
Lanham, MD 20706
www.rowman.com

Distributed by NATIONAL BOOK NETWORK

British Library Cataloguing in Publication Information available

Library of Congress Cataloging-in-Publication Data
Names: Wommack, Linda, 1958– author.
Title: Colorado's historic schools / Linda Wommack.
Description: Essex, Connecticut : TwoDot, 2022. | Includes bibliographical references and index. | Summary: "Part regional history and part travel guide, featuring over 140 of the most significant schools across the state, all recognized as historic landmarks. Along with interesting school stories and building descriptions, there are historic photos and stories of legendary teachers, tragedies, and even murder over the 150-year history of Colorado's schools"— Provided by publisher.
Identifiers: LCCN 2022012151 (print) | LCCN 2022012152 (ebook) | ISBN 9781493062904 (paperback) | ISBN 9781493062911 (epub)
Subjects: LCSH: Schools—Colorado—History. | Education—Colorado—History. | Historic buildings—Colorado.
Classification: LCC LA246 .W66 2022 (print) | LCC LA246 (ebook) | DDC 371.009788—dc23/eng/20220316
LC record available at https://lccn.loc.gov/2022012151
LC ebook record available at https://lccn.loc.gov/2022012152

∞™ The paper used in this publication meets the minimum requirements of American National Standard for Information Sciences—Permanence of Paper for Printed Library Materials, ANSI/NISO Z39.48-1992.

Contents

Foreword

There's no one more fitting to write the tales of Colorado's pioneer teachers and the schools where they taught than historian Linda Wommack. Linda has been writing about the history of her home state for more than twenty years. I'm sure her love of history was fostered, in part, by an amazing Colorado teacher.

The stories of the brave women who traveled from the East to teach on the western frontier are diverse and compelling. From the Catholic sisters who helped initiate schools in remote areas of the Southwest to Protestant evangelical ladies who established schools on Indian reservations to women educators who sacrificed personal comfort and risked their lives to bring the joy of learning to children beyond the Mississippi. Their efforts did as much to settle the Wild West as did celebrated lawmen, gold seekers, and the railroad.

The harsh conditions of the western territory did not dissuade these women. Many had already endured hardships. The War between the States, floods, crop failures, family tragedies, and the needs of their own communities prompted numerous women to pursue careers in education. For many, their yearning to teach extended outside their own sphere of influence. They wanted to take their talent to uncharted territories and make a difference in the lives of those who needed them most.

Many pioneer women teachers were well educated. They had backgrounds of culture and were widely read. Some had traveled extensively. Some had made distinguished contributions to prestigious publications. For others, their background in the field had been relegated solely to teaching their numerous siblings how to read and write. They were poor women who had never ventured outside the small towns where they had been raised. All shared the same conviction, however: to train the minds and build the characters of students living in a rugged new land. They dared to inspire their pupils with noble visions and challenged them to realize those dreams and aspirations.

Some of these teaching pioneers operated the first schools in rugged and tough locations where lawlessness was commonplace. Others were the first or sometimes the most distinguished teachers of special subjects such as music, the "gentle home arts," manners and morals, and physical education for women. Others were librarians and teachers of handicapped children.

Colorado's Historic Schools has done a great service in calling attention to the wonderful achievements of the women teachers in the Centennial State and in celebrating the charm of the buildings that were the center of learning for many eager students.

Chris Enss
New York Times best-selling author

Introduction: Back to School Days

When Horace Mann was elected to the Massachusetts Board of Education in 1837, he used his new position to launch a major educational reform. He enacted the common school movement, ensuring that every child could receive a common education funded by local taxes. With overwhelming support, the new education system was a huge success, and Horace Mann became known as the "Father of the Common School." The influence of this successful school program soon spread to other states, where it was equally successful. Within twenty years it had spread west to US territories. Mann wrote:

> *Without undervaluing any other human agency, it may be safely affirmed that the Common School may become the most effective and benignant of all forces of civilization.*

The history of Colorado's schools dates to 1859, when Owen J. Goldrick established the first school in Denver City. On October 3, 1859, Goldrick began teaching thirteen students in a one-room log cabin. When Colorado Territory was created in 1861, Goldrick served as the first superintendent of what would become Denver Public Schools. While Goldrick is the first male instructor, Miss Indiana Sopris became the first female teacher when she opened a private school in a log cabin on the corner of Fourteenth and Market Streets.

As Colorado's population grew and settlers established rural homes, farms, and ranches, schools were being built across the state. Under Colorado Territorial government, school districts were formed with a ruling body consisting of a president, a secretary, and a treasurer. According to a History Colorado article, "Rural School Buildings in Colorado Multiple

Many students traveled to school on horses. CARNEGIE LIBRARY FOR LOCAL HISTORY–BOULDER

Property Submissions," "Schoolhouses were often no more than two or three miles apart [as] parents did not want their children traveling too far or traversing dangerous terrain." Thus, many children walked or rode their horses each day. Rural teachers often boarded with a local family for the school term and returned to their own family during the summer, the growing months for farmers. These schoolhouses were often the social centers of the community. Civic town meetings as well as other political events were held there.

Within twenty years, in 1876, Colorado achieved statehood, and with it the first school of higher education was established: the University of Colorado at Boulder. Throughout Colorado's history, schoolhouses have played an important role. Through the halls of education have been romance, scandal, controversy—even murder—all of which can be found in the pages of this book.

The schools listed are all on the Colorado State Register of Historic Properties; many are also on the state's Landmark Preservation list. The first State Register listings occurred in 1991 and the National Register two decades earlier. Other schools included are on the Colorado Endangered Places list.

The majority of the historic photographs are from the archives of the Denver Public Library, and I am indebted to photo archivist Coi E. Drummond-Gehrig. Other photos came from various historical societies, town museums, and interested folks who volunteered to share their photos for this work.

I am indebted to the various historical societies, community groups, museums, and enthusiasts who helped with this project. Colorado Landmark Preservation and Colorado History Center are at the top of that list. Kenneth Jessen of Loveland contributed his vast knowledge as well as photographs, as did Teri Johnson, Christie Wright, and the Park County Historical Society. Others include Charles Tribbey, Sherry Skye Stuart, Charlotte Bumgarner, Mark Perdew, Greg Fuller, and Heath Gay.

Thank you, one and all.

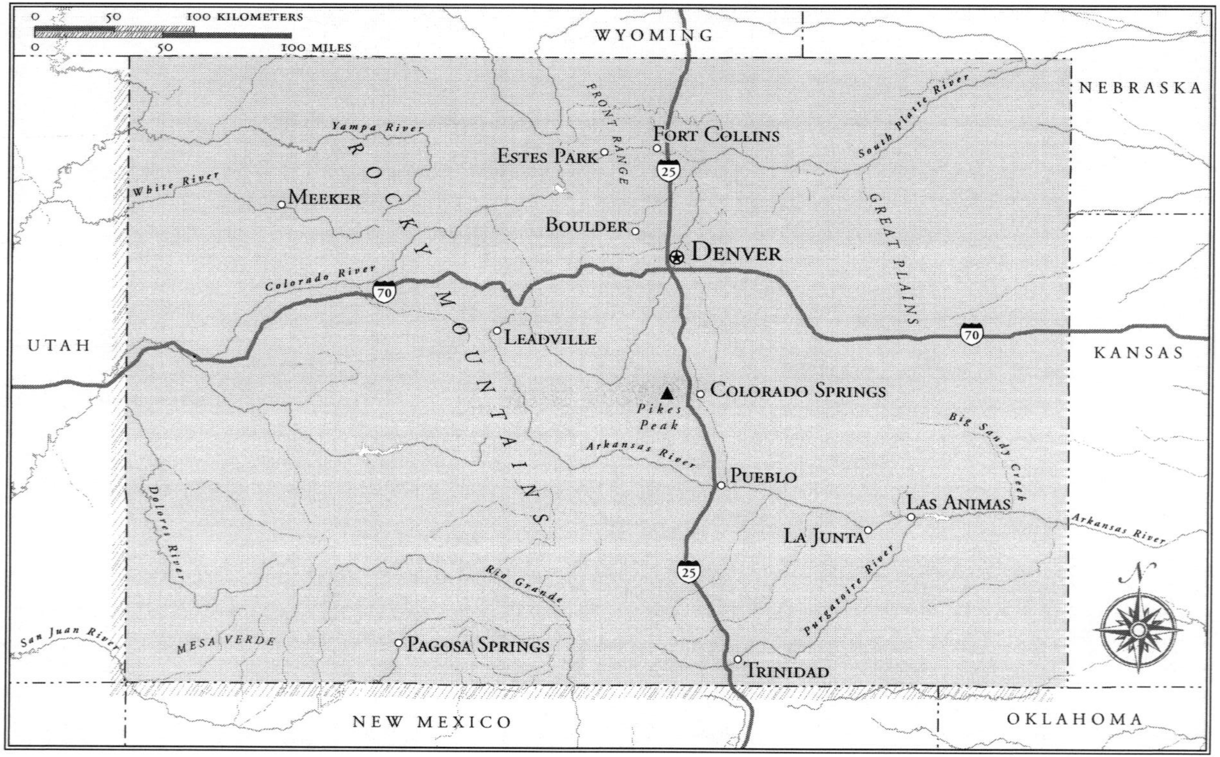

0 50 100 KILOMETERS
0 50 100 MILES
WYOMING
NEBRASKA
UTAH
KANSAS
NEW MEXICO
OKLAHOMA
Yampa River
ROCKY MOUNTAINS
FRONT RANGE
ESTES PARK
FORT COLLINS
25
South Platte River
White River
MEEKER
BOULDER
DENVER
GREAT PLAINS
Colorado River
70
LEADVILLE
COLORADO SPRINGS
Pikes Peak
Big Sandy Creek
Arkansas River
PUEBLO
LAS ANIMAS
LA JUNTA
Dolores River
Rio Grande
Purgatoire River
N
San Juan River
MESA VERDE
PAGOSA SPRINGS
TRINIDAD

COLORADO

The Eastern Plains

Chapter One

Hi Ho! Hi Ho! It's Off to School We Go

Counties South of Interstate 70

Baca County

The **Springfield Schoolhouse** (281 West 7th Ave., Springfield) was built in the town of Springfield in 1889. Architect M. Gaffney constructed the building, located on the northeast corner of Seventh and Tipton Streets, using entire blocks of local sandstone for the walls. Gaffney hired a stonemason and local workers, paying them a dollar a day for their work. Their work was impressive, including a front-gabled roof and recessed windows. When completed at a total cost of $2,000, the citizens fondly referred to the building as the "Rock School." When the Springfield Schoolhouse closed in 1921, the building served as the community center. Later, the local chapter of the Masons acquired the building and transformed it into a Masonic temple.

Bent County

In the agricultural town of Las Animas in Bent County, the **Bent County High School** (1214 Ambassador Thompson Blvd., Las Animas) was built in 1914. The building was designed by James Larson and built by the La Junta architectural firm of Dubree, Walter, Larson & James. The foundation, basement, and center front steps to the entrance were constructed of native stone. The exterior featured elements of the Classical Revival style, including four symmetrically placed windows at the basement level as well as the first and second levels of the structure. The center entrance of the building was noted in the State Register of Historic Properties for "its imposing, three-story, massive-columned architecture."

The historic school is also noted for three public figures who attended Bent County High School. Famed author James Michener's wife, Mari Sabusawa, attended the school. Ken Curtis, who became a Hollywood actor most noted for his role as Festus in the television series *Gunsmoke*, graduated from the school in 1935. Another graduate of Bent County High School was Llewellyn Thompson, who later became the US ambassador to the Soviet Union, becoming an expert in Russian politics. Thompson went on to serve President John F. Kennedy during the 1962 Cuban Missile Crisis. The street where the school is located was later renamed Ambassador Thompson Boulevard in his honor.

In 1939 the school property was expanded to include two additional buildings, the **Las Animas Junior High School** and the **Las Animas Middle School**. A project of the federal government's Works Progress Administration (WPA), the additions were constructed in the new Moderne style of the era.[1]

Bent County High School served the area until 1998, when student enrollment fell drastically. The school was closed and sat vacant for the next ten years. In 2004 Bent County received a $96,000 grant from the Colorado Department of Public Health and Environment for removal of asbestos and pigeon guano. Today Bent County High School and the two additional school buildings continue to receive additional restoration efforts for eventual repurposing proposals.

Cheyenne County

On the windswept plains of eastern Colorado is the ghost town of Aroya. The town's misspelled name comes from the Spanish word *arroyo,* which means "dry gully." It was a stage stop on the Smoky Hill Trail and then a railroad stop for the Kansas Pacific Railroad in 1869. At about that same time, Bohemian immigrant and Civil War veteran Joseph Ottmar Dostal came to Colorado with the intent to sell meat to the hungry miners on their way to the gold hills of the Rockies. Dostal's J.O.D. Ranch was just a few miles east of town. As the town grew in population, largely due to the success of the J.O.D. Ranch, a small school was built to serve the learning needs of the community's children.

A few years later the entire town burned down. It was rebuilt three miles east, near Dostal's ranch and where the railroad line crossed the often-dry Big Sandy River. A new depot was constructed where west-bound passengers could board and stagecoaches would bring passengers east, 130 miles from Denver, a three-day journey at the time, to what was now christened "Arroyo City." Homesteaders came and stayed. Farms and ranches were built, as well as fine homes in town. A small piece of land with a sloping hill just west of town was donated for the new school building.

The one-room **Aroya Schoolhouse** (the junction of US Highways 94 and 40/287, Aroya) was a fine example of work done by local handymen. The hipped roof gradually rose to an open bell tower. A large flagpole was erected on the grounds. Separate privies for girls and boys were located behind the school. Inside, there were rows of desks and a stove for heat. Perhaps the most curious feature are the two entrances, one at each end of the front corners of the school. The two entrances were in keeping with the Eastern custom of separate entrances for girls and boys. As time went on, this impractical custom faded in the West. The tall arched doorways give the illusion that the building is oval rather than square. It was considered an architectural wonder at the time.

The town peaked in the 1920s and quickly faded following the stock market crash of 1929. When Interstate 70 was constructed in the 1960s, the highway allowed more and more travelers to bypass the town. Over the years, businesses closed, the buildings were torn down, and many people moved away. A few businesses remained, and some early farmers and ranchers stuck it out, including the J.O.D. Ranch. The Aroya School stayed open until the early 1960s, when school consolidation was occurring across the state. After the closure, the school was consolidated with Kit Carson School in Kit Carson, Colorado, twenty-two miles east of Aroya. One of the many students at the Aroya School was Carl Beverly "Bev" Bledsoe, who was born in Aroya in 1923. Bledsoe went on to represent his hometown district as a state congressman. He became speaker

The Aroya Schoolhouse sits abandoned on the eastern plains
GREG FULLER PHOTOGRAPHY

of the State House of Representatives, a position he held longer than any other Coloradoan in the state's history.

Today the Aroya School is abandoned and on private land. Pictures taken from the road make it one of the most photographed schoolhouses in the state. It is on Colorado's Most Endangered Places list.

Approximately eighteen miles east of Aroya is the town of Wild Horse, a hub along the Union Pacific Railroad line in today's Cheyenne County. Established in 1869, the town was named for nearby Wild Horse Creek, where a large herd of wild horses roamed. The **Wild Horse School** (8513 US Hwy. 40/287, Wild Horse) was built in 1912. The clapboard building included three windows on either side of the double-doored entrance. Following the closure of the schoolhouse in 1964, the building served as the community center.

Also in Cheyenne County, the town of Eads lays claim to a historic school-related structure. In 1929, the **Eads School Gymnasium** (West 10th and Slater Streets, Eads) was built on the northeast corner site of the town's massive complex of school buildings and sports fields. The one-story Mission Revival–style building was designed and built by Colorado Springs architect Elmer Ernest Nieman. Nieman's plans called for the building to be fireproof, one of the first in the state. A ceremony for the laying of the cornerstone was held on March 19, 1929. The *Kiowa County Press* covered the event and wrote: "If in many years to come the building is torn down, this record will be of great interest. The black granite stone indicates A. W. Hinds served as superintendent and school board members included Fred W. Eder, George B. Black, and J. C. Miller. Architect E. E. Nieman's name is also inscribed." Built atop a concrete foundation, the building was constructed of variegated magnesium pressed brick in various shades of yellow. Contrasting brown brick was used in the foundation as well as to surround the windows and entrance. The original window glass was embedded with chicken wire.[2] The metal roof included a gabled arch over the entrance.

The new Eads School Gymnasium opened in time for the fall school term on October 7, 1929. The facility provided physical education classes as well as training and coaching of the athletic teams of the Eads school district, including basketball, football, gymnastics, track, volleyball, and wrestling. In the 1930s school athletic programs included girls' programs such as basketball and volleyball. The Eads School Gymnasium served the school needs of the community, particularly after the local high school burned down in 1937. During the Great Depression the gymnasium building served as the community center and provided hot lunches and fresh milk not only to the students but to many residents as well.

Today the Eads School Gymnasium still provides athletic support to the children of the Eads community. Students in kindergarten through fifth grade use the gym for their sports curriculum. Practice sessions for junior and senior high athletes also are held at the facility.

Crowley County

The town of Crowley is the county seat of Crowley County, named for State Senator John Crowley in 1911. The **Crowley School** (301 Main St., Crowley) was constructed in 1914. Built in the Second Renaissance Revival style, the one-story schoolhouse included trios of round arched windows and an arched double-door entrance. Other architectural details were double-sided concrete stairs leading to the entrance and a raised basement with small square windows. Perhaps the most elaborate detail was the large cupola above the entrance, which rose to support the ornate wood-shingled bell tower. After nearly seventy years of service, the school was closed in 1980. In 1994 the building was restored and opened as a museum, community center, and municipal facility. The Crowley School is not only the oldest public building in the town but also the finest example of the type of architecture in Crowley County and possibly the state.

Just a block away, **Crowley Consolidated High School** (200 Main St., Crowley) was constructed in 1920. The two-story brick building was built with a T-shaped plan that included a gymnasium in the back.

Huerfano County

In 1912 the Archdiocese of Denver approved the addition of a school on the property of the St. Mary Church and School in Walsenburg. Built in the Mission Revival style, the two-story building with a raised basement was constructed of red brick. Round arched windows enhanced the exterior as well as the three entrances. When the building was completed a year later, the construction cost $25,000. Today the **St. Mary School** (121 and 201 East 7th St., Walsenburg) is a historic portion of the St. Mary Church complex.

The **Huerfano County High School** (415 Walsen Ave., Walsenburg) was built in 1920. The architectural firm of Isaac Hamilton Rapp and William Mason Rapp constructed the three-story building in red brick. Elements of the Collegiate style included the square corners, rectangular windows, and a protruded entranceway. After fifty years as a high school, the building became the Walsenburg Middle School.

Kit Carson County

In the agricultural community of Flagler is the **Second Central School** (404 4th St., Flagler). Built in 1915, the schoolhouse was originally located some thirteen miles southeast of the town. After school district consolidations in 1959, the school was closed and remained vacant for several years. In 1993 the historic schoolhouse was moved into the town and refurbished as a museum.

Las Animas County

The agricultural community of Kim, southeast of Springfield, was established in 1893 by Olin D. Simpson on a portion of his homestead. Simpson named it Kim for popular novelist Rudyard Kipling's boy hero. The **Kim High School and Elementary School** (425 State St., Kim) were

Students ready to start their day. DENVER PUBLIC LIBRARY

built in 1939 as projects of the WPA program. Built of local sandstone, both two-story brick school buildings matched in architectural design. In the center of the school complex, a hip-roofed gymnasium served as the sports center for both schools. The three buildings, constructed over an eight-year period, provided much-needed employment in the town during the Depression years. When completed, the school building complex was dedicated in a special ceremony in January 1941. Today the school buildings still serve the students of Kim; the gymnasium is utilized by the community as the Kim Activity Center.

Prowers County

The small agricultural community of Alta, in Prowers County, was established eleven miles north of the Arkansas River. The **Hopewell School**, a wood-framed building erected in 1890, served the educational needs of the area's students. C. B. Kell was the first teacher, followed by Miss Emma Martin.[3] Three years later, in 1893, the Alta Vista school district was formed, consolidating three districts. The new **Alta Vista School** was constructed the same year at a cost of $1,400. When completed, the one-room clapboard schoolhouse had twenty-three students, taught by Miss Ellen Strain. As this was the beginning of the 1893 economic depression, the Alta Vista School was the first in the state to institute a formal lunch program.

In 1917 a new school building was constructed. The two-story, red-brick structure was built in the Mission Revival style, and the windows were double-hung with wooden frames. The entrance featured metal double doors with an arched window above. Inside, there were three classrooms, a lunchroom that also served as an auditorium, a library, and administrative offices. The first teacher was paid $38 a year to teach the thirty students. The **Alta Vista School** (8785 CR LL, Lamar) is one of very few historic schools still serving the educational needs of its students. Several additions have been built over the years, and today the building is known as the Alta Vista Charter School, serving students from kindergarten through sixth grade. It is the only charter school in the county, and the last rural schoolhouse preserved and still in use.

Just a few miles directly south of Alta was the town of Hartman. In 1938 the **Hartman Gymnasium** (School Avenue, Hartman) was built with funds from the WPA, as well as other New Deal programs available in Prowers County. Located next to the Hartman School, the gymnasium served as the sports center for the students until 1980, when the school closed. The Hartman City Council voted to demolish the school building in the name of progress but retained the Hartman Gymnasium structure. Today the historic building serves the community as a social center.

In the northwest corner of the county is the agricultural community of Wiley. The town was named for William M. Wiley, president of the local Holly Sugar Company. In 1938, the Works Progress Administration constructed an adjoining building to the existing Wiley single-story schoolhouse. The natural stone building included double windows on either side of the double-door entrance, trimmed with narrow limestone. Large wrought-iron hinges enhanced the double-door entrance. The new building, known as the **Wiley Rock Schoolhouse** (603 Main St., Wiley), provided classrooms for instruction in agriculture and homemaking. A soundproof music room was utilized for band and orchestra instruction. An adjacent building provided hands-on instruction in blacksmithing. This historic school building is associated with the list of New Deal Resources of Colorado's Eastern Plains, as well as listed on the National Register of Historic Places.

Approximately ten miles southeast of Hartman and four miles west of the Kansas border is the town of Holly. The **Holly Gymnasium** (North Main Street, Holly), which took three years to complete, was a project of the Works Progress Administration. Construction of the building began in 1936. The exterior of the building was erected with Niobrara, a chalklike stone native to the area. When completed in 1939, the gymnasium was the first in Holly. The new building also served as the lunchroom and an area for band and orchestra practices.

Otero County

The town of La Junta in Otero County claims a very historic school property. In 1914 Walter Dubree was commissioned to build the **North**

La Junta School (located on the corner of Main and Trail Streets) just north of the Arkansas River. The two-story red-orange brick building was set atop a raised basement constructed of concrete. Curiously, the enclosed porch entrance had two doors: one for boys and one for girls.

Notes

1. New Deal Resources on Colorado's Eastern Plains, National Park Service.
2. National Register of Historic Places Registration Form, June 18, 2013.
3. Ada Betz, *A Prowers County History* (Lamar, CO: Prowers County Historical Society, 1986), 370.

Chapter Two

Towner School Bus Tragedy

In 1931 the small community of Towner, located ten miles west of the Kansas border in Cheyenne County, experienced a horrific school tragedy. On the morning of March 26, a strong wind out of the north created a blizzard that swept the southeastern plains of Colorado. On that fateful day, Carl Miller, the school bus driver, made his usual route around Kiowa County and delivered twenty-two children at the Pleasant Hill schoolhouse. Miller and the two teachers, Maude Moser and Franz Freiday, noticed a drastic change in the weather. As the students had only their lunch and nothing else, the teachers insisted that Miller return the children to their homes. Miller argued that the students would be safer at the schoolhouse, but as the storm blew harder, the teachers insisted.

It was approximately 9:00 a.m. when Miller loaded the students, including his own daughter, seven-year-old Mary, back onto the school bus and left the school property. The Towner school bus was a 1929 Chevrolet truck with a wooden school bus body attached to the bed. Wooden benches served as seats for the children.[1] Miller turned the bus left, traveling southwest, although he could barely maneuver down the snow-blown road. Finally Miller managed to turn the bus around in or near the road, thinking it best to return to the schoolhouse. By this time the windshield had frosted over and Miller could barely see. When the bus got stuck in a barrow ditch on the west edge of Holly-Towner Road, it was only three miles from the schoolhouse when it stalled out.

What happened next is a story of both heroism and tragedy. According to the surviving children, Carl Miller fixed the bus as best he could against the storm. He then encouraged the children to play inside the bus in an obvious effort to keep them moving in the freezing temperature, as well as to keep their minds occupied. As evening approached, Miller built a small fire inside a five-gallon milk can, burning pieces of wood from the bus and schoolbooks to keep the children from freezing to death.

As the older children led the younger ones in singing and playing games, thirteen-year-old Rosemary Brown knew they were in terrible trouble. Her little brother, Bobby, said he was hungry. The lunch pails were frozen to the bus floor, the lids compacted with ice. There was no food. Little Laura Huffaker had to go to the bathroom. Her sister Alice told her to go in her panties. At least that would keep her warm, Alice thought.

Night fell and the temperature dipped. Miller insisted on singing, dancing, boxing—anything to keep the children awake. To sleep was to die. And so the children sang, jumped, boxed, and danced throughout the long, frigid night. Morning finally dawned, dreary, freezing, and still snowing. Miller ordered exercising once again. As his daughter Mary slowly got up and Louise Stonebraker refused to get up, Miller must have noticed the glazed-over look in Louise's eyes and grabbed her out of the seat.

Miller knew he had to go for help. He left Maxine Brown and Eunice Frost in charge, with instructions to keep themselves and the children moving. Miller left the bus and promised to return with help. Looking around the bus, deciding what to do, Eunice's gaze stopped at Louise Stonebraker. Louise's eyes stared blankly from where she leaned against the back seat of the bus. Louise was dead. Blanche Stonebraker, Louise's sister, later recalled that moment and said from then on, one by one, the children died. Each body was taken to the back of the bus and placed next to Louise's frozen body.

Clara Smith urged the others into exercising. The air grew thick, and the bus floor was icy. Rosemary Brown noticed her baby brother, Bobby, mumbling. She slapped him but his eyes just stared vacantly ahead. She put him on her lap and rubbed him, crying as she felt his body go limp. Eventually, Bryan Untiedt lifted Bobby from Rosemary's lap and laid him next to Louise in the back of the bus. One by one the remaining children began to go into shock. They exercised; it became an obsession. Someone noticed little seven-year-old Kenneth Johnson staring and mumbling, "Daddy will come; Daddy will come!" Clara Smith grabbed him, but he crumpled to the floor. He too was dead. Clara carried him to the back of the bus.[2]

As night fell, physical and emotional exhaustion set in. Mary Louise Miller had no strength left to move and could no longer remember how long ago it was that her father had gone for help. Bryan's little brother, Arlo, wanted to sleep, but Bryan kept slapping him. Bryan and Charley Huffaker, the two oldest boys, tried to go out in search of the road, landmarks, anything. The snow hit their faces hard, and the brightness hindered their eyesight. They couldn't see anything past an arm's length. The wind was so fierce, they could barely stand. Afraid they would get lost, they went back to the bus.

Bryan held his little brother, Arlo, and rubbed is hands and legs. Clara saw the same hollow stare in Arlo as in the others, and she watched in horror as it crept over Bryan as well. Someone said it was getting warmer. Bryan looked around. It was getting dark; how could it be getting warmer? Yet everyone said it was true, and soon Bryan began to feel the warmth as well.

Charley Huffaker thought he heard horses. Someone else heard horses' hooves clomping on the frozen ground. Soon everyone heard them, and then a great gust of freezing air came into the bus. The children sobbed and cried; they had no energy for anything else. Breaking the door open, Bud Untiedt and Dave Stonebraker began carrying the children off the bus. There were seventeen survivors.

And so, thirty-eight hours of survival and death aboard a stranded school bus ended. But the tragedy was not over. The children were taken by buckboard to the nearest farmhouse. As Bud Untiedt carried his son Arlo to the buckboard, Dave Stonebraker carried others. His daughter Louise was left on the bus beside Bobby and Kenneth.

At the small Reinhart home, a half mile from the bus tragedy, blankets were found as child after child was brought in and laid on the floor. Fern Reinhart had little food but plenty of potatoes. As potatoes fried, she rubbed feet, hands, and limbs in an effort to warm the children. Edwin Reinhart left for the Stonebraker farm, the only farm in the area with a telephone. A doctor was needed, and quickly. As the word got out, neighbors trickled in to help. Some brought food, blankets; someone even brought whiskey. As the children warmed under the blankets, they began to thaw out. Men massaged the limbs with snow and salt, and as the prickling, stinging sensation led to pain from the severely frostbitten limbs, the children were each given a tablespoon of whiskey. The rubbing of the children's limbs continued.

Bryan Untiedt knelt beside his father as he tried to revive his younger son, Arlo. Bryan cried when he realized his little brother was dead, and told his father that he had only slapped Arlo to keep him awake. By nine o'clock that night, Mary Louise Miller had also died.

Dr. F. E. Casburn and other citizens from Holly traveled by car through the deep snow all night, reaching the Reinhart farmhouse in the

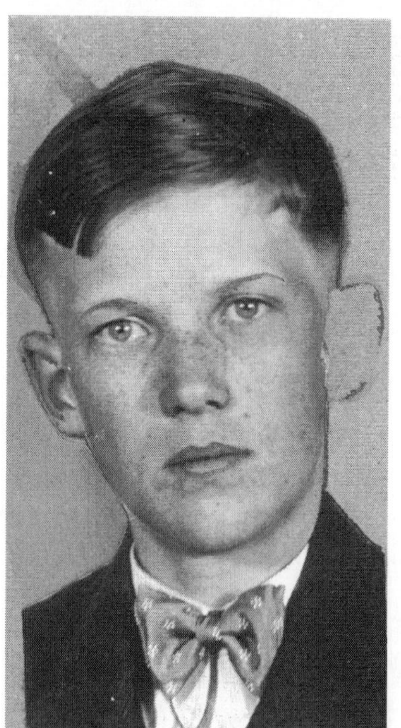

Bryan Untiedt helped save his fellow students from freezing to death in a deadly blizzard. DENVER PUBLIC LIBRARY

early-morning hours. By morning the storm was over. A group of the men from Holly set out for the Towner bus to retrieve the three bodies. Along the way they discovered the body of bus driver Carl Miller. His frozen body was approximately a half mile off the school road, along the barbed-wire fence. Evidently Miller had found the barbed-wire fence and followed it as a guideline. Although he was wearing gloves, they had torn, and his hands were covered in frozen blood from the cuts he had received from the wire before he froze to death.

The following day, Saturday, March 28, Dr. Lemly Hubener of Tribune, Kansas, arrived at the Reinhart home. After examining the children and consulting with Dr. Casburn, the two physicians recommended that the children be moved to a hospital as soon as possible. Lamar Mayor Charles Maxwell, operator of a private hospital in his city, offered the facility for the care of the children. Maxwell contacted Jack Hart, a local

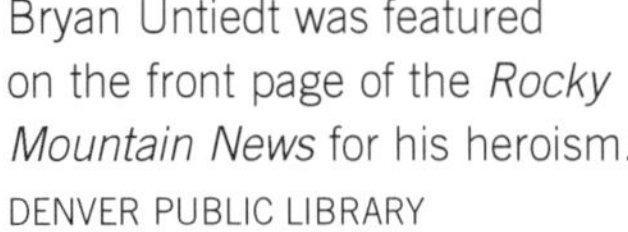

Bryan Untiedt was featured on the front page of the *Rocky Mountain News* for his heroism.
DENVER PUBLIC LIBRARY

pilot, to fly a few of his nurses to the Reinhart home and then return with the children to the hospital in Lamar. It was a small plane, so it required several trips.[3]

Dr. Napoleon M. Burnett, a specialist in frostbite care, personally treated all the children. Under Dr. Burnett's care, none of the children suffered permanent damage. As the surviving children recuperated from frostbite at the Lamar hospital, a quiet, solemn funeral was held for the six dead children, with burial at the Holly Cemetery.

The horrific story of the Towner bus tragedy made national headlines. From the *New York Times* to the *Denver Post* and *Rocky Mountain News* and west to the *Los Angeles Times*, the sad story of the Pleasant Hill School students gripped the nation.

On October 7, 1931, nearly seven hundred local citizens gathered at the Holly Cemetery for a ceremony dedicating the placement of a tall carved stone obelisk near the graves of the victims of the school bus tragedy. Led by several Colorado lodges, including the Odd Fellows, a time capsule that included newspaper clippings and photos was placed in the base of the monument.

Notes

1. Pleasant Hill (Towner) School Bus Tragedy Intensive Research Plan, 2012. Colorado History Center.
2. Ibid. See also: Secrest, *Children of the Storm.*
3. Pleasant Hill (Towner) School Bus Tragedy Intensive Research Plan, 2012. Colorado History Center.

Chapter Three

Frontier Teacher Sister Blandina Segale

The Colorado frontier of the nineteenth century was filled with adventure. It was an open landscape where dreams awaited those who dared. One such dreamer was Sister Blandina Segale, an unlikely pioneer and a force to be reckoned with.

Born Rose Maria Segale in Cicagna, Italy, in 1850, she immigrated to America with her parents and three siblings in 1854 at the age of four. Living in Cincinnati, Ohio, young Rose Maria attended public school and Catholic church services. From very early on, she knew she wanted to serve the Church. After completing school, she entered the convent at St. Vincent Academy. On December 8, 1868, seventeen-year-old Rose Maria Segale took her sacred vows and was given the name Sister Blandina.[1]

By all accounts, Sister Blandina excelled in her new duties. She taught children at the local Catholic school, conducted Bible studies at the church, volunteered to help the needy, and gave her time to elevate the poor. She had often prayed to be sent out west to Santa Fe, where her order, the Sisters of Charity, had set up a parish in 1865. Her prayers were answered in 1872 with her sudden and unexpected summons to work on the western frontier. Although thrilled to finally fulfill her dream, she was also sad to leave her many Sister friends as well as her older sister, Maria, who was also a nun. Sister Blandina promised to keep a journal of her experiences for Maria (now Sister Justina). Sister Blandina kept this journal for twenty-one years, the only account we have of her personal experiences.

Sister Blandina Segale was a courageous prairie schoolteacher. DENVER PUBLIC LIBRARY

Twenty-two-year-old Sister Blandina boarded the train in Steubenville, Ohio, heading for Kansas City. There the strong-willed and fearless nun boarded a cargo train loaded with railroad supplies and only one coach car for passengers. The otherwise boring trip was highlighted by an unexpected stop due to a herd of stampeding buffalo.

At the time, the train rails went as far into southern Colorado Territory as the small town of Kit Carson. From there it was another four days' travel by stagecoach to Trinidad. At the Otero and Sellar Stage Line, Sister Blandina was welcomed by the agent's wife, Mrs. Mullen. The following morning she covered the floor of the stagecoach with clean hay to keep Sister Blandina's feet and ankles warm. After a warm meal, she helped the nun into the coach, wrapping her in a large quilted blanket.

Meanwhile, Mr. Mullen had readied the stagecoach for the long, rough ride. Unlike the new state-of-the art Concord stages, this stagecoach had no springs; every flap was tied down, and the wheels were well greased for winter travel. The stage traveled along the treacherous Santa Fe Trail, struggling over the rocks and ruts at an average of twelve miles per hour.

Finally, on December 10, after twelve days of overland travel, Sister Blandina arrived in Trinidad (present-day Las Animas County). Stepping off the stage at the adobe mercantile store of M. Wise and Company, the nun observed her new home. Dirt streets, busy with horses and wagons, were the least of her worries. In no time at all, she learned about the lawless, gunslinging, gambling town that was Trinidad. Sent here to establish a Catholic school, the good Sister must have been overwhelmed. Even so, she took the challenge head-on. Shortly after her arrival, Sister Blandina wrote a letter to her sister. Dated December 10, 1872, it included the following passage:

> *My dearest dear, Here I am safe in Trinidad, Colorado Territory, instead of in the island of Cuba where we first thought I was to go. No wonder this small pebble is known as the sister of the Far West.*[2]

In no time at all, Sister Blandina's warm personality and youth won over the community of Trinidad. With charitable fundraising and generous donations from influential members of the community, a handsome adobe schoolhouse was built, debt free. Sister Blandina always considered the Mount San Rafael School her finest accomplishment. The cheerful nun took her place before her first group of students, and in true form she recounted the experience of teaching boys nearly her age and much taller. In a journal entry dated January 10, 1873, she wrote:

> *Today my capacity for controlling them was put to the test. You know I'm a companion outside of the schoolroom, and a teacher the instant the threshold of the schoolroom is crossed.*

Sister Blandina took a personal interest in eradicating the extreme crime of Trinidad, and the citizens trusted her for it. She single-handedly confronted a lynch mob to ensure a fair trial for an accused killer and prevented a coal mine disaster with the help and friendship of local Native Americans. Sister Blandina was also instrumental in raising money for the new Mount San Rafael Hospital.

Yet Trinidad history will forever recount the tale of Sister Blandina and Billy the Kid. Legend says, as these things often did with the good Sister, that a student came to her in confidence. The youngster had wandered into the aftermath of some sort of gunfight. One of Billy the Kid's gang members had been shot in the thigh. Unable to travel, the other members of the gang prevailed on the youngster for help in hiding their pal. This the boy did, hiding him in a nearby adobe hut. Eventually it was learned that the shooting had happened over a dispute at Dick Wooten's tollgate on the Raton Pass road.

After several attempts by the boy to get a doctor's help, he finally went to the one person he knew he could trust—his teacher, Sister Blandina. Immediately the good sister went with the boy to the hideout. Sister Blandina realized that the bullet had gone through the leg, so she dressed the wound with fresh bandages. For more than a month she attended the injured outlaw's wound on a daily basis. She also brought food and fresh linens and provided spiritual inspiration in a way only Sister Blandina could. Everyone around the hut called her patient "Happy Jack." However, in a private moment, the patient confided to the nun that his real name was Bill Schneider.

He also told her that Billy the Kid would be coming in the next day or so. Schneider said Billy was coming to take him back to New Mexico, but first the "Kid" would kill the four doctors of the Trinidad area for not helping him. Stunned, to say the least, the good Sister didn't alert the authorities but instead relied on her instincts and inner faith. Sticking with her routine, Sister Blandina arrived at the hideout. At her patient's bedside, Schneider introduced her to the shy young man standing by the bed with his finger tapping his holstered gun. From Sister Blandina's journal:

> *He has steel-blue eyes and a peach complexion. One would take him to be seventeen—innocent looking, save for the corners of his eyes, which tell a set purpose, good or bad.*

Sister Blandina also recounted in her journal that Billy the Kid politely thanked her for all she had done and said, "It would give me pleasure to be able to do you any favor." The nun took his hand and gratefully accepted his offer. She asked that he not seek vengeance against the doctors of the community. The Kid immediately granted the favor, saying, "The favor stands. Not only that, Sister, anytime my pals and I can serve you, you will find us ready."

The grateful nun shook the Kid's hand, never to see him again. Although there is no evidence to corroborate Sister Blandina's account of meeting Billy the Kid, we can speculate that her actions saved the lives of four of Colorado's doctors that day: Michael Beshoar, Palmer, and the Menger brothers. Not long after her encounter with the outlaw, Sister Blandina was transferred to Santa Fe and later to Albuquerque, New Mexico. After twelve years she returned to Trinidad in 1889. She was pleasantly surprised to find the town had "lost its frontier aspect." She wrote in her journal:

> *The remaining men who were ready at the least provocation—or that of strong drink—to raise the trigger have settled down to domestic infelicity.*[3]

Sister Blandina's journal and subsequent book reveal the many struggles she not only endured but conquered. In 1892 Sister Blandina faced an obstacle in her teaching career that she refused to give in to. Members of the Trinidad school board requested that the nun no longer wear her black habit while teaching. Sister Blandina wrote:

> *The board said it was "inappropriate" for a public school and "brings us into trouble."*

She refused to abandon her nun's habit and soon left Trinidad for Pueblo, where she became principal of the St. Patrick School. Her final journal entry for the Trinidad years reads:

> *Adios, Trinidad, of heart-pains and consolations!*

After a year in Pueblo, Sister Blandina returned to her hometown of Cincinnati, where she died at the age of ninety-one on February 23, 1941. Her tireless work in Colorado did not go unnoticed. In 1958 Denver's Regis College posthumously awarded Sister Blandina the Civis Princeps (First Citizen) award in education.

NOTES

1. Segale, Sister Blandina, *At the End of the Santa Fe Trail.*
2. Ibid.
3. Ibid.

Chapter Four

If You're Happy and You Know It, Clap Your Hands

Counties North of Interstate 70

Morgan County

In 1911 the **Knearl School** (314 South Clayton St., Brush) was built in the town of Brush, in Morgan County. The two-story brick building with a central entrance and gabled roof was a simple design typical of small early twentieth-century civic buildings. The Knearl School offered classes to students from first through third grade, primarily for the benefit of immigrant families, beginning with the Germans and later the Latinos who worked in Morgan County's sugar beet fields. The Knearl School building is the oldest surviving schoolhouse in Brush, serving the area for more than sixty years before consolidation forced its closure.

The town of Brush hosts another historic school. The respected Denver architectural firm of Montjoy & Frewen was contracted to design and build the **Central Platoon School** (411 Clayton St., Brush). The two-story brick building was built in the Italian Renaissance style, featuring symmetrically placed windows, terra-cotta trim, and an arched door. Construction was completed in 1928, and the school enrolled its first students. This educational institution was one of the first in the state to adopt the experimental platoon form of student learning. This system assigned students to a set curriculum in which they attended assigned classes in separate rooms taught by individual teachers.

The Knearl School in Brush. CHARLES TRIBBEY

The Central Platoon School was the first of its kind in the state. CHARLES TRIBBEY

In 1909 the **Lincoln School** (914 State St., Fort Morgan) was built in the town of Fort Morgan, county seat of Morgan County. Designed in the Mission style, its prominent feature was the curved gable over the school entrance. Other features included a brick stairway to the entrance and a hipped roof. The Lincoln School served the elementary students of Fort Morgan for the next fifty-three years. With the addition of the kindergarten curriculum adopted nationwide in 1962, the school administrators included the new students in their educational system. A much-needed addition was built in 1920, nearly tripling the school's size. The addition included a gymnasium, complete with a stage for plays and recitals. Today the Lincoln School, one of four elementary schools in Fort Morgan, continues to educate young students in the community.

In the town of Hoyt, also in Morgan County, the residents built a simple clapboard building in 1918 that became the **Hoyt School** (3515 Road B, Hoyt). During the Great Depression years, the Works Progress Administration (WPA) constructed an addition to the school. The main

The Lincoln School in Fort Morgan is the town's only school with historic designation. CHARLES TRIBBEY

floor featured a stage at the front of the classroom and stairs leading to a basement in the new facility. This addition was a standard inclusion of the New Deal federal relief program instituted by President Franklin D. Roosevelt. The basement addition included a fully functioning kitchen used to provide hot lunches for the students. The adjoining larger room served as the cafeteria where students ate. The Hoyt School also served as a community center where social dances, potluck dinners, and local elections were conducted.

At the western edge of Morgan County is the historic **Old Trail School** (421 High St., Wiggins). The rural one-room schoolhouse was built in 1912 for the students of the Wiggins community and surrounding area. The building was moved twice during its service and again when student consolidation caused closure of the school. The schoolhouse is also listed with the Rural School Buildings in Colorado.

The Old Trail School in Wiggins is one of the state's oldest clapboard schoolhouses.
CHARLES TRIBBEY

Sedgwick County

In the extreme northeast corner of Colorado, Sedgwick County, named for Gen. John Sedgwick, was created in 1889. In 1925, when the Great Western Sugar Company built a large sugar beet plant in the county, the town of Ovid, named for founding father Newton Ovid, was founded. Located just north of the South Platte River and four miles west of Julesburg, the town prospered for several decades.

In 1928 noted Denver architect Temple Buell designed the **Ovid High School** (300 Morgan St., Ovid). Buell incorporated elements of the Art Deco style in the two-story building. Constructed of blond brick, the double-door entrance was graced with three rectangular windows above. The Ovid High School, the only example of Art Deco architecture in the county, remains in service to area students.

Weld County

Greeley, the county seat of Weld County, was established in 1870. In 1895 Denver architect Harlan Thomas received the contract for Greeley's first high school. Built of red-pressed brick, the two-story **Greeley High School** (1412 14th Ave., Greeley) included a raised basement. Elements of the Georgian Revival style were evident in the round-arched windows and a single-story extended apsidal bay at the back of the school building.

In 1902 Denver architect Robert Roeschlaub designed and built the adjoining **Greeley Grade School**. Constructed atop a red sandstone foundation, the two-story elementary school was also built of red-pressed brick and trim to match the high school edifice. Roeschlaub's crowning achievement was the connecting passage between the two buildings. In 1982 both former school buildings were renovated into professional offices.

With Greeley's growing population, a new high school was commissioned in 1927. Denver architect William N. Bowman and Greeley architect Sidney G. Frazier worked together to design and build the new **Greeley Central High School** (1414 14th Ave., Greeley). Constructed in the Gothic Revival style, the three-story brick structure included a series of triple windows and an arched entrance. The school is still in use today.

Sidney G. Frazier, Greeley's highly respected architect, was also contracted to construct the **Greeley Junior High School** (811 15th St., Greeley). The project was funded through the government's Works Progress Administration, part of President Franklin D. Roosevelt's New Deal program. Completed in 1938, the Greeley Junior High School is the only example of the Art Deco style in Greeley.

On April 1, 1889, Colorado Governor Charles S. Thomas signed a bill creating the State Normal School, an institution designed to train qualified teachers for public schools throughout the state. Greeley citizens raised the needed funds to build a school building. A groundbreaking ceremony and laying of the cornerstone was held on June 13, 1890. The building was completed in the fall, and the State Normal School opened on October 6. Ninety-six students enrolled in the teacher training program, with four instructors. Teaching certificates were earned following completion of the two-year program.[1]

In 1911 the name of the school was changed to **Colorado State Teachers College** (501 20th St., Greeley), and the school was expanded by the state legislature. This was also the year the school began offering four years of undergraduate work as well as a Bachelor of Arts degree. The name of the academic institute was again changed in 1935, to the Colorado State College of Education, in order to establish the new graduate program. The final name change occurred in 1970, when the institution became known as the University of Northern Colorado.

Over the years the original college land on Rattlesnake Hill grew to more than one square mile. Many buildings, primarily designed in the Collegiate Gothic or Neoclassical style, are now on the historic preservation lists.

The 1907 Carter Hall, designed by Frederick W. Ireland Jr., served as the campus library. Constructed of blond brick, the building features Neoclassical elements, including curved two-story reading rooms and a terra-cotta entrance. In later years it was converted into offices as the administration building. Ireland was also responsible for constructing the Faculty Club House in 1930, a three-story structure built in the Tudor Revival style.

The main building of the University of Northern Colorado at Greeley. DENVER PUBLIC LIBRARY

In 1913 James Murdoch designed the four-story Neoclassical Guggenheim Hall for industrial and fine arts classes. Next to this building Murdoch erected a matching structure known as Crabbe Hall, named for John G. Crabbe, the college president at the time.

Belford, Decker, and Gordon Halls were women's dormitories built in 1921 by William B. Ittner of St. Louis, Missouri.

These historic buildings are included as part of a Multiple Property Submission on the National Historic Register.

The **Daniels School** (Colorado Highway 60 and Weld County Road 25, Milliken), also in Weld County, is one of many fine examples of Colorado's rural school buildings. Located near the town of Milliken, southwest of Greeley, the historic schoolhouse sits just north of US Highway 60. When School District 21 was established in 1873, dairy farmer James Daniels donated an acre of his land for a school building. The first was a wood-frame structure that served as the schoolhouse until 1911. At that time the school district sold the building, which was moved off the property to make way for the new building. Constructed in 1911 by C. J. Mathers and H. W. Richmond, the single-story building was built in the Classical Revival style. Red brick was used for the exterior, accented with beige sandstone. Rectangular windows were added, as well as two smaller windows flanking the entrance. Five concrete steps led to a porched entrance with four Tuscan columns and two Tuscan pilasters. A pediment with the date "1911" and the words "School Dist. 21" was placed on the wall of the porched entrance. The hipped roof supported a bell tower with four wooden columns and a tall spire.

The double doors opened into the vestibule, which led into the single classroom. A unique feature of this one-room schoolhouse was a pull-down partition with wainscoting "counter-weighted like a double-hung window," which was in the center of the room.[2]

Just a few yards west of the schoolhouse, a teacherage—a separate building for teacher counseling—was also built. The single-story clapboard building was erected atop a concrete foundation. Horizontal wood drop siding covered the exterior. A wood-frame screen door and wood-paneled door offered entrance to the dwelling. The interior consisted of a living space, one bedroom, and a small kitchen. Behind each building was a brick outhouse with two seats.

The opening of the 1911 school term was delayed by a month because supplies needed to complete the project were delivered later than expected. The *Milliken Mail* reported on the opening of the new school in its September 22 issue:

> *The school term opened in the Daniels district, Monday, with JTR Miller again presiding. The delay in the opening of the term was owing to the new schoolhouse not being finished before. The new building is a very creditable structure for a new district school.*

The Daniels schoolhouse faced possible closure in 1919 when several parents advocated for consolidation with Milliken District 64, as it was closer to where those families lived. In a vote conducted in the spring, the proposed consolidation failed. The *Milliken Mail* ran an editorial in the May 5 issue:

> *According to the vote Saturday at the Danials* [sic] *school district some seem to think that they can get along without the help of this district in educating their children. Well they have had a chance anyway.*

Nevertheless, the 1919 school term ended on a positive note for students and their parents. The *Milliken Mail* reported on the event in the May 19 issue:

> *The Danials* [sic] *school gave their closing exercises last Thursday evening to a large and appreciative audience. The children did splendidly and showed much good training. Friday was the culminating day in the children's eyes, when the mothers brot* [sic] *loads of good things for a fine lunch, to say nothing of the huge freezer of ice cream which was excellent and just touched the spot.*

On October 19, 1959, School District 21 was finally consolidated and annexed to District 64. The historic Daniels School closed its doors to student education, and the schoolhouse and property reverted to the Daniels family. Today the schoolhouse and teacherage remain on the Danielses' private property, but the buildings are visible from the road. The two outhouses were removed in the 1930s and replaced with two wood-framed, two-seated privies, constructed by the WPA.

In 1882 Benjamin H. Eaton established the town of Eaton near the Denver & Pacific Railway tracks in Weld County, northeast of Greeley. Eaton, who became governor of Colorado in 1885, believed that the availability of a school and strong student attendance were not only a positive measure for the town but also an investment in the future. In 1909 the first Eaton High School was built, named in honor of the town's founding father and former governor.

By the 1920s, due to the establishment of a sugar beet factory, the town's population doubled. School enrollment nearly doubled as well. Teachers held classes in the basement, in hallways, and even on the stairwell landing.[3] In 1929 a new **Eaton High School** (114 Park Ave., Eaton) was designed by Robert Kenneth Fuller and built in the Collegiate Gothic style. The two-story blond-brick building featured tall rectangular windows on both floors flanked by an arched double-door entrance. The high school underwent an extensive restoration in 1996 thanks to a $300,000 grant from the Colorado Historical Society. During the restoration process, Eaton resident Charles Fugua observed the progress with a personal interest. He pointed to a second-story opening on the north side, and said: "I remember one time when the math teacher looked out the window and caught me and my buddies ditching study hall."

Four miles north of Eaton, the **Ault High School** (208 West 1st St., Ault) was built in 1921. Prominent local architect Sidney G. Frazier constructed the three-story building with local red brick, enhanced with blond brick. The double-door entrance featured an elaborate decorative arch. In 1976, after fifty-five years of service as a high school, the building became the Ault Junior High School. The school closed in 1992 and remained vacant for several years. When the Board of Education considered demolishing the building, community outrage led the board members to reconsider. With grants from the Colorado State Historical Fund, an extensive renovation of the building began in 1999. Today the historic Ault High School building once again serves the educational needs of the town's students as part of the Highland Middle School campus.

Early-days classroom. CARNEGIE LIBRARY FOR LOCAL HISTORY–BOULDER

Approximately seven miles southeast of Keensburg, in the southern portion of Weld County, is the small agricultural community of Prospect Valley. In 1903 the **Prospect Valley School** (33318 Hwy. 52, Keensburg) was built. The two-story brick schoolhouse received an addition in 1920 and was expanded again in 1940. The school is still in use today.

In 1927 Robert K. Fuller designed and built the **Brighton High School** (830 East Bridge St., Brighton). In 1955 the building became the Brighton Junior High School. Today the building serves the community as the Brighton Heritage Academy. The school is listed on the State Historic Register.

Notes

1. University of Northern Colorado archives.
2. National Register of Historic Places Registration Form for Daniels School, dated February 21, 2005.
3. Fogelberg, *Colorado History NOW*, August 2001 issue.

The Front Range

Chapter Five

The Farmer in the Dell

Counties along Interstate 25 South

Adams County

Henry J. Mayham, a philanthropist from New York City, arrived in Colorado in 1890. At the area of Crown Point, the highest point in the central Front Range, Mayham envisioned a university campus. After purchasing 600 acres, Mayham met with Reverend T. H. Hopkins of the Denver Presbyterian Church. Convincing the reverend that the site was ideal for a Presbyterian college, the two formed an alliance to create a college campus. Reverend Hopkins organized a board of trustees and was instrumental in the incorporation of the Westminster University of Colorado in 1891. That same year, Mayham hired Stanford White, an esteemed architect with the Denver firm of H. H. Richardson, to design and construct the college building.

White constructed the three-story building in the Richardsonian Romanesque style. The edifice was built of red sandstone from the Manitou Springs area. A three-story square tower at the center of the building included an arched entrance. Two tall towers graced the corners of the front portion of the building. The exterior of the building was completed in 1893 just as the financial panic that began that year crippled the state and halted construction. Construction resumed in 1907. The interior contained several classrooms, an auditorium, and administrative offices.

Westminster University opened in 1908. For several years the university struggled with low enrollment. During World War I the university

The imposing Westminster University. DENVER PUBLIC LIBRARY

accepted only male students, despite the fact that far more males were enlisting to fight the war rather than attending college. In 1920 Westminster University was purchased by the Pillar of Fire Ministries for $40,000. However, the Presbyterian Church retained the rights to operate a seminary, which included the Belleview Christian School, and the broadcasting rights of KPOF, the oldest religious broadcasting station in the state.

Today the historic **Westminster University** (3455 West 83rd Ave., Westminster) building is the towering pioneer landmark in the community of Westminster.

In this same area of Adams County, the **Pleasant DeSpain School** (7200 Lowell Blvd., Westminster), named for early settler Pleasant DeSpain, was built in 1892. The one-story schoolhouse, built in the Romanesque Revival style, represents the beginning of elementary child education in the community. The beige brick building received an addition in 1926 that included indoor plumbing and restrooms. Pleasant

DeSpain School, today known as Harris Park School, still serves the educational needs of Westminster students.

The agricultural town of Westminster, established in 1911, was appropriately named for the area's landmark, Westminster University. In 1929 E. B. Gregory designed and built the **Union High School** (3455 West 72nd Ave., Westminster). The two-story building was constructed of local blond brick. In 1939 the school district hired an architect to construct an additional wing, which increased the number of classrooms. An adjoining gymnasium was built with funding provided through the Works Progress Administration. The Union High School was closed in 1949. Today the building serves as an alternative education center.

Arapahoe County

Further east, Arapahoe County, which adjoins Denver County, hosts three historical schoolhouses. The **Cherry Creek Schoolhouse** (9300 East Union Ave., Greenwood Village), a one-room clapboard structure built in 1874, is the oldest building in the city of Greenwood Village. It was moved to the campus of Cherry Creek High School in 1951.

In 1914 the **Curtis School** (2349 East Orchard Rd., Greenwood Village) was built. The one-story building was constructed of brick with rough-faced sandstone trim. The hipped roof supported a central belfry. Today the historic schoolhouse serves as the city's Cultural Arts Center.

In 1950 the rural town of Melvin in Arapahoe County was flooded following construction of the Cherry Creek Dam. Fortunately, the Cherry Creek Valley Historical Society stepped in to save the town's 1922 schoolhouse from being submerged. The **Melvin School** (4950 Laredo St., Aurora) was moved three miles away to a portion of the Smoky Hill High School campus. Restoration of the building took place in 1978, and a replica of the original square bell tower was erected.

In March 1864, Territorial Governor John Evans founded the Colorado Seminary. A devout Methodist, Evans had also founded Northwestern University in his home state of Illinois before being appointed territorial governor of Colorado by President Abraham Lincoln. Evans believed that Christianity must be an intrinsic part of education, as it was a direct foundation for developing strong character. However, many of

Evans's supporters, who became trustees of the institution, were intent on creating an institution of learning that was open to all. This was reflected in the official charter of the school, which stated: "No test of religious faith shall ever be applied as a condition of admission."[1] For several years after its founding, the seminary struggled financially and actually closed for a time. In 1880 the trustees of the school reorganized and opened the school with a new image and a new name, the University of Denver. The school, under the direction of Chancellor David Hastings, was located in a small building in downtown Denver. In 1884 John Hipp became the first graduate.

At that time, university administrators began looking for property to build their own school building and expand the institution. It took years, but finally, in 1889, Rufus "Potato" Clark, a successful farmer who lived some seven miles south of downtown Denver, donated a portion of his land to the university. After fundraising efforts, they broke ground for the **University of Denver** campus (2199 South University Blvd., Denver), located at what would become the corner of East Evans Avenue and University Boulevard.

In 1890 Denver's renowned architect Robert Roeschlaub constructed the first of many buildings that would eventually grace the university campus. At the heart of the campus, University Hall was constructed

The University of Denver was founded in 1864 as the state's first private institution of higher learning. DENVER PUBLIC LIBRARY

in the Romanesque Revival style. The cornerstone of the red sandstone building was exactly one mile above sea level. A stone porched entrance was graced with circular stair towers on either side. A central bell tower was erected atop the pitched roof. In 1892 the **Iliff School of Theology**, named for wealthy cattle rancher John Wesley Iliff, was founded as a seminary and school of religious studies of the University of Denver. The cornerstone of Iliff Hall was laid on June 8, 1892, at 2201 South University Boulevard. The three-story building was erected atop a raised basement of natural sandstone. A double-sided stone stairway led to the arched entrance. Above the entry an arcade of eight Gothic arched windows reflected the Richardsonian architectural style. Also in 1892, Humphrey Barker Chamberlain, a wealthy real estate agent, donated a parcel of land adjacent to the university campus as well as a monetary sum to the administration for construction of an observatory. Robert Roeschlaub built the structure using natural red sandstone. Gabled wings enhanced the building, as did a protruding arched entrance. A pediment with Chamberlain's name carved into it was placed over the entrance.

The economic depression of 1893 greatly affected the university. By the fall term of 1894, student enrollment had dropped to just over two hundred pupils. That year the school was more than $100,000 in debt. Chancellor William F. McDowell consolidated several departments, dropped a few others, and paid professors' salaries at irregular intervals based on available funds. As the depression went on, the administration was faced with selling undeveloped portions of the campus to meet their financial obligations. Chancellor McDowell later remarked on the financial difficulties: "The depression was a swift storm that came and went, leaving devastation in its wake. It was sudden enough in its coming, but showed no haste in its departing."[2]

Despite McDowell's efforts, the university's debt grew. McDowell resigned in June 1899, and Professor Herbert A. Howe became interim administrator. The university's financial difficulties were alleviated significantly by Rufus Clark, who had originally donated a portion of his farmland to the university in 1889. Ten years later, in May 1899, Clark sold another tract of land, near today's Downing Street and Yale Avenue, for $60,000, a portion of which he donated to the university.[3]

In February 1900 Henry Augustus Buchtel, pastor of Trinity Methodist Church, agreed to take over the leadership of the fledgling University of Denver. Buchtel, known as a visionary and an exceptional fundraiser, was installed as the university's third chancellor on February 5, 1900. During his twenty years as chancellor, Buchtel not only managed to relieve the debt of the university through fundraising and favorable donations but also made the institution profitable and reestablished the university's reputation as a respectable institution of higher learning. In 1913 the Buchtel Memorial Chapel was erected on the campus in his honor. Sadly, a 1917 fire gutted the chapel, although the tower was saved and remains on the campus as a memorial.

Over the years, many additions and improvements were made to the university campus. In 1932 the Mary Reed Library was built. The library was constructed of red sandstone, matching the original buildings. Margery Reed Hall, named for Mary's daughter, was built in 1939.

In 1960 the Evans Memorial Chapel, located at the corner of Thirteenth and Bannock Streets, was moved to a pristine location on the campus of the University of Denver. The 1874 brown rhyolite chapel, designed in the Gothic Revival style, was the cornerstone of the Grace Community Methodist Church. The building of the chapel was commissioned by Territorial Governor John Evans, in memory of his daughter, Josephine Evans Elbert, who had died earlier that year. The Evans Memorial Chapel served the Methodist community until 1959. That same year, many buildings of the Grace Community Methodist Church were dismantled or destroyed in the name of "progress." Fortunately, the Evans Memorial Chapel was saved.

Today the University of Denver remains Colorado's oldest private institution of higher education. As of this writing, two former Colorado governors, Richard Lamm and William "Bill" Owens, are among the teaching faculty. The historic buildings are on the Colorado State Multiple Listing Register as well as the Colorado State Multiple Listing Register.

In 1864 the Sisters of Loretto arrived in Colorado Territory at the invitation of Bishop Joseph Machebeuf, Denver's first Roman Catholic bishop. Shortly thereafter, the Sisters opened St. Mary's Academy in a two-story frame house on California Street. One of the academy's students was Mary Louise Bonfils, who joined the order at fourteen. In 1882, on her thirtieth birthday, Mary was appointed Mother Superior of St. Mary's Academy. Mother Pancratia Bonfils, as she became known, began soliciting support and donations from bankers and businessmen to build a facility to board the academy's growing student population.

Mother Pancratia selected a location in the southwestern suburb of Sheridan Heights, seven miles southwest of downtown Denver. The Sisters of Loretto were so taken by the hillside location and the panoramic view that they agreed to purchase forty-five acres for $16,000. Mother Pancratia and Sisters Bartholomew Nooning, Victorine Renshaw, and

Historic Loretto Heights was first a school for Catholic girls.
DENVER PUBLIC LIBRARY

Agatha Wall were all in full agreement that the magnificent site would become home to a new Catholic school and would be called Loretto Heights. The *Colorado Catholic Register* printed the following in the July 11, 1899, issue:

> *Stand on the sloping hill on which the building is situated, Denver and the Valleys of Bear Creek and the Platte with their glint of silver water at your feet. Beyond are the mountains, piled blue and gold, crowned with white snow. In all Colorado, my eyes have not lighted on a fairer picture. It will be [the] finest edifice of its kind west of the Mississippi River.*

And it was. That year Denver's premier architect, Frank E. Edbrooke, was contracted to build the new Catholic school for girls. Edbrooke employed the Richardsonian Romanesque style in his construction of **Loretto Heights** (3001 South Federal Blvd., Denver). The four-story structure, built of native rough red sandstone from the Manitou area, included a stoned entry arch with a statue of the Blessed Virgin Mary in a grotto placed above. The cross-gable roof included dormers enhanced with carved stone crosses on each end. The most prominent feature, which remains an iconic landmark to this day, was the six-story center tower that included a stone-pillared observatory. A bell tower capped with a slate roof supporting a large cross completed the iconic tower. The 1865 bell, which originally hung in St. Mary's Academy on California Street, was rehung at Loretto Heights.

As construction progressed, the *Denver Republican* reported the details of the new school on the front page of the paper dated May 20, 1891:

> *The corridor extends the full length of the building's 200 feet and there will be a tower, 30 feet square and 165 feet high, from the ground to the top of the cross. There will be 86 principle* [sic] *rooms and a wing to wing veranda on every floor. The building will be heated with steam and lighted by electricity from private plants on the grounds.*

Today, Loretto Heights serves the community in a variety of ways.
AUTHOR'S COLLECTION

The interior of the building included the above-mentioned corridor with walls of wainscoted oak. The thick oak floor was enhanced with one-inch colored hexagonal tiles that formed snowflake designs. The hall led to a library, recreation rooms, laboratories, and classrooms. The second floor housed the Sisters' dormitory, an infirmary, and restrooms. In the basement were the kitchen, dining hall, and bathrooms. When completed in the spring of 1891, the total construction cost was just under $200,000.

On November 2, 1891, twenty nuns and fifty students boarded the Circle Train in Denver, traveled by rail the seven miles to the west station, and then walked the last two miles to the new school. For the next few days there was no electricity or water because the contractor had neglected to turn on the utilities. During that time seventy more pupils arrived. On June 15, 1892, a ceremony for the first graduating class of Loretto Heights was held. The two graduates were Katherine Casey and Olive Fort.

Over the years, education programs were added as women's roles in society dictated. In 1918 a college curriculum was offered to the students, and a Teacher Education program was formed in 1926. By 1948 the administration had completely phased out the elementary and intermediate programs. That year, Loretto Heights became an accredited four-year college for women.

In summer 1988, Loretto Heights College closed and three of the academic programs, including the teachers and nursing programs, moved to Regis College. A year later, the Teikyo University Group purchased the former Catholic educational institution. This group was formed by Dr. Shoichi Okinaga and included thirty international institutions by the time the group expanded in Colorado. In 2009 the Teikyo University Group opened Colorado Heights University on the same property.

Denver's South High School was the final school included in Mayor Robert Speer's "City Beautiful" plan. South High School began much like East High School, as a product of pioneer Professor Owen J. Goldrick's Union School. As Denver's south side was less populated than the other quadrants, this area did not get its own school building until 1893. At that time, Grant Elementary School was built at the corner of Washington Street and Mexico Avenue.[4] In 1894 thirty-five students utilized two classrooms in this building. In 1907 the Grant building could no longer accommodate the growing student population. A new building was erected next to the Grant School, which unofficially became known as South High School.

With a robust economy during the 1920s, more businesses were established in South Denver and population increased as well. By 1924, enrollment at Grant/South High neared eight hundred students, more than the building could accommodate. Fortunately, in 1924 Grant School was officially renamed the **Denver South Side High School** (1700 East Louisiana Ave., Denver) when the institution was selected to become part of Mayor Robert Speer's "City Beautiful" plan. The site selected for the new school was in South Denver, next to Washington Park. Brothers Alan, Arthur, and William Fisher of the architectural firm Fisher and Fisher were contracted to design and build the new school.

On October 31, 1924, a ceremony was held at the site for laying the cornerstone. Items placed in the cornerstone included an American flag, a Bible, a copy of the US Constitution, a copy of Denver's city charter, and signatures of the school's first teachers and students.[5] Fisher and

South High School enjoyed landscaped grounds as a part of "City Beautiful."
DENVER PUBLIC LIBRARY

Fisher designed the building in the Italian Romanesque style. Arthur A. Fisher, who was fond of stone carvings and sculptures, employed sculptor Robert Garrison to create several stone statue designs, making South High School possibly the most artistically designed structure among Denver's public schools. The main entrance, constructed at the historic cornerstone, was enhanced by a tall tower that included a three-foot-tall gargoyle sculpture, which became the symbolic protector of South High School. Over the north entrance, Garrison created a bas-relief sculpture representing the tree of knowledge and young scholars. Extravagant carvings enhanced the exterior of the three-story, redbrick building from the arched north entrance to the corner pillars. The school's north court featured four stone-carved winged lions. The most prominent feature of the building was the tall, square clock tower enhanced with intricately carved cornices. Garrison also continued his stonework inside the school. The large study hall features sculptures of birds representing positive qualities for students, including an owl for wisdom, a crowing rooster for punctuality, a parrot for attentive learning, and a penguin symbolizing positive behavior.

The boys' gymnasium, later renamed the North Gym, included a balcony for additional seating during basketball games and other indoor sports. During the 1950s several changes were made and new additions constructed, including an auxiliary gymnasium and locker rooms for the girls. These improvements were originally planned in the 1940s but were delayed by World War II.

Notable alumni of South High School include John L. Hall, 1952, Nobel laureate; Albert Mooney, 1924, founder of Mooney Aircraft Company; and Nicholas Willhite, 1959, pitcher for the Los Angeles Dodgers from 1963 to 1967.

Broomfield County

Eighteen miles north of Denver in the small agricultural community of Westlake, a school was built for the area's children. The original one-room clapboard schoolhouse was replaced in 1902 with a fine two-story brick building. The main floor consisted of a large multipurpose room and smaller offices, while the three classrooms were on the second floor. The **Westlake School** (13005 North Lowell Blvd., Broomfield) served the educational needs of children from first through eighth grades. In those early years, nearly all the students were involved with the local 4-H club. The boys raised a variety of farm animals, while the girls were involved in domestic projects such as cooking, baking, and sewing. Following eighth grade graduation, the students attended high school in Lafayette, their tuition paid by the school district.

After a few years of operation, teachers Mr. and Mrs. Brown were hired by the school district. The couple moved into living quarters in the basement of the schoolhouse. The Browns were instrumental in initiating a hot lunch program, and several mothers of the students volunteered to bring the hot meals to the school.

In 1952 the Westlake School was closed, as it did not meet fire protection codes.

Denver County

In the summer of 1859, Professor Owen J. Goldrick arrived in the bustling supply town of Denver City. Within a few weeks of his arrival, the twenty-six-year-old Goldrick rented a small one-room, leaky log cabin with a sod roof at McGaa and F Streets (today's Market and 12th Streets). It was there, on October 2, that Professor Goldrick opened the first school in Denver. The *Rocky Mountain News* ran an editorial in its October 20, 1859, issue:

> *Our Union School—We are glad to notice this modest but important institution is prospering beyond the sanguine expectation of its friends. Professor Goldrick is prepared to teach the young. It already numbers some twenty pupils, and more have been promised. The grades range from the little ones, just learning their a–bs, to those in Reading, Writing and the useful branches of Arithmetic, English Grammar, Geography &c.*

Professor Goldrick's little log cabin schoolhouse was not only the first in Denver but also became the foundation for the Denver Public School system. The *Denver Evening News* ran a related article in the October 16, 1860, issue under the headline "Free Schools in Denver":

> *Our readers, by referring to the official report of the proceedings of the Council on Saturday, published in our paper yesterday, will be gratified to see that action has already been taken by that body to secure as early as possible, the establishment of one or more free schools in our city.*

When Professor Goldrick was appointed the first superintendent of schools, he divided the Denver City area into five districts. The first two districts were divided by Cherry Creek, with District 1, East Denver, obviously on the east side of the creek, and District 2, West Denver, on the west side. The Central district was in the downtown area, and the North and South districts were divided by the South Platte River. The *Rocky Mountain News* printed the following in the April 29, 1865, issue:

The regular annual district meeting for the first School District, Arapahoe County, will be held in the rear room of the News office, on Monday the 1st day of May, A. D. 1865, at 2 o'clock p.m. for the purpose of electing board members for the district.[6]

In an effort to provide a school for their students, the citizens of West Denver were able to raise $700 to purchase the vacant Arsenal Building at Larimer and today's Eleventh Street. The two-story brick building had stored federal military supplies and ammunition during the Civil War. With this purchase in late 1865, the Eleventh Street School became the first in the five districts to own their schoolhouse. A maximum capacity of two hundred pupils were educated at the facility until the eighth grade. In 1880 the Central High School was built near Kalamath and Tenth Streets. The new school originally accommodated students from first through twelfth grades. Due to the unprecedented population increase in the 1880s, the Central School could no longer serve the needs of West Denver's students by 1883. The following year, Franklin School was constructed at West Colfax Avenue and Mariposa Street. On June 13, 1884, the graduation was held at 2:00 p.m. That first graduating class included Frances Brandt, Laura Duccy, Effie Hallam, Charles McDonough, Morrison Stillwell, and Lelia Williams.[7] In 1901 the proud citizens of West Denver quickly dubbed the school Denver West High School, as it became the second high school in the Denver Public School system.

During Robert Speer's term as mayor of Denver, the four Denver high schools, North, East, South, and West, became part of Speer's "City Beautiful" plan. Elegant park designs and elaborate public buildings were a major part of Speer's grand design, and he insisted that the four directional high schools be associated with a major park in each of the four district quadrants. In 1926 architect Frank Edbrooke was hired to design and build the new **Denver West High School** (951 Elati St., Denver). The school's principal, Harry V. Kepner, assisted Edbrooke in his design for the school. On March 26, 1926, a dedication ceremony was held at the site of the future school. In keeping with Speer's "City Beautiful" plan, the land chosen for the new high school overlooked Sunken Gardens and Speer Boulevard.

Denver's Franklin School, later called Denver West High School. DENVER PUBLIC LIBRARY

General contractor William Tamminga was in charge of the construction. Constructed in the English Collegiate Gothic style, the blond-brick building also included elements of the Neo-Gothic style. The most prominent feature in this style was the 110-foot central tower, complimented with two smaller towers on either end. Inside the enormous building, spacious halls led to sixty-five classrooms. The auditorium, which seated nearly 12,000, was the pride of the school.

Over the years, West High School received several improvements and additions. In 1974 a redbrick building was added to the west side of the school and housed the gymnasium. In 1978 a new academic center opened. The two-story building had science labs and classrooms on the first floor and music rooms on the second floor. In 1990 a district-wide bond initiative provided funds for a swimming pool and an outdoor patio, which was connected to the main school building via a three-story bridge.[8] In 2002 a two-story state-of-the-art library was erected. Dedicated on April 19, 2002, the library featured four large bay windows. In 2012 the historic high school was renamed West Leadership Academy in an effort to better prepare students for college.

The Ashland School, built in the Highlands neighborhood in 1872, was the precursor to North High School. The original one-room schoolhouse was replaced in 1883 with a new brick structure and a new name, Denver North Side High School. It was the first Denver Public school to officially use a directional name. One teacher was hired to teach the students, ranging from first through twelfth grades. In 1886 the first graduating class was entirely female, with a class grade average of 98.

In 1911 a new **Denver North Side High School** (2960 North Speer Blvd., Denver) building was built to accommodate the growing student population. Bordering Highland Park, the three-story brick structure is Denver's best example of the Beaux Arts style in academic buildings. Denver architect David W. Dryden included ornate arched pillars, Ionic columns, and arched windows and doors. When completed, the new high school included one hundred rooms and cost the taxpayers $335,000. During Mayor Speer's "City Beautiful" project of the 1920s, the city and county of Denver deemed North High School "large enough and beautiful enough that it did not need to be replaced."[9]

Denver's North High School was part of Mayor Speer's "City Beautiful" plan.
DENVER PUBLIC LIBRARY

Notable alumni of North High School include Prime Minister of Israel Golda Meir and Colorado historian Caroline Bancroft.

In 1885 the **Emerson School** (1420 Ogden St., Denver) was designed and built by Denver's most prominent architect, Robert S. Roeschlaub. The two-story redbrick building was the first in Denver to incorporate an in-house library for the students. Emerson School was also the first to offer a student council and host the new Parent-Teacher Association (PTA). Several years after the school closed, the building was acquired in 1980 by Capitol Hill Senior Resources Inc. For a time the building was renamed the Frank B. McGlone Center. Later, the group donated the building to the National Trust for Historic Preservation. In 2010 the preservation group began a $2 million renovation of the building. Today the former Emerson School houses offices for the Historic Denver group as well as Colorado Preservation Inc.

The Emerson School is the oldest schoolhouse in Denver.

The **Corona School** (846 Corona St., Denver) is another example of esteemed architect Robert S. Roeschlaub's work. In 1889 Roeschlaub constructed the two-story brick building atop a raised basement. At each end of the structure, square corner towers graced the edifice, topped with bell-shaped domes. The interior included classrooms on both floors. An elaborate central staircase led to the second-floor classrooms. In 1938 the school was renamed the Dora Moore School in honor of the school's principal, who had served in that position for thirty-five years.

In the 1990s the building underwent a renovation that included the addition of a three-story brick building. Years later, when the empty building had suffered from neglect and faced demolition, the Denver Landmark Preservation Commission stepped in, designating the school as its first historical landmark school building.

David W. Dryden was a notable Denver architect known for his work with Denver school buildings, including North High School. In 1901 Dryden became the supervising architect for Denver's School District No. 1, a position he held for twelve years. Three years into his term, Dryden took on the project of a new school building. In 1904 the **Evans School** (1115 Acoma St., Denver) was built. The three-story, redbrick building included a portico and a large copper-clad cupola. The Evans

Denver's Corona School was later renamed the Dora Moore School in honor of a respected former principal. DENVER PUBLIC LIBRARY

School was the first in Denver to accommodate physically handicapped, blind, and deaf students. The Evans School served as an elementary school for nearly seventy years before closing in 1970.

One of Denver's oldest Catholic schools, the **Sacred Heart School** (2830 Lawrence St., Denver) was built in 1890. The solid brick building was constructed in the Romanesque Revival style. Classrooms were located in areas of the building so as to optimize natural lighting and ventilation. The Catholic school served as a high school until 1939, when it became an elementary school. The school was noted for its centrally located auditorium and gymnasium, and these facilities were also available to the community. The Sacred Heart School closed in 1979, one year short of celebrating ninety years of serving Catholic students.

The history of **Denver East High School** (1545 Detroit St., Denver) started where the city itself began, near the confluence of the South

Platte River and Cherry Creek. In 1868, Amos Steck donated two lots on the north side of Arapahoe Street between Seventeenth and Eighteenth Streets to the City of Denver for a school building. On February 11, 1870, the Territorial Legislature passed legislation to provide for school funding and to allow a citizen vote for "A Board of School Directors." Denver School District No. 1 was created that same year from this legislative act.[10] The new Board of School Directors purchased two lots adjoining Steck's donated lots; a year later, three more lots were purchased at a cost of $2,000. On January 11, 1872, the Arapahoe Street High School was built at a cost of $90,000. The school district's first high school, it was also the first to provide access to the city library.

After nine years the school building fell to the progress of downtown commerce. As Denver's economy grew, the school property became valuable commercial land and was sold in 1881 for $165,000. A new high school was built farther east, at Nineteenth and Stout Streets, and renamed the Stout Street School. Denver architect Robert Roeschlaub, known for his work with Denver schools, designed the new school.

Roeschlaub's plan included carving the face of a young girl into the cornerstone of the new school. It was to be a symbol of the administration's dedication to the city's youth. Roeschlaub held a beauty contest in an effort to find a model for his carving. He selected six-year-old Ella Matty, who was said to have "the face of an angel."[11]

The three-story brick building and its grounds encompassed one entire block and could accommodate seven hundred students. Over the years the school became known as East Side High. By 1921 this building had also outgrown the student population.

As part of Mayor Speer's "City Beautiful" project, land was purchased along the City Park Esplanade, which bordered the south side of City Park. Denver architect George Hebard Williamson, an 1893 graduate of "Old East High," was hired to construct the new East High School building. When the Old East High building was demolished, the cornerstone with the carving of "the face of an angel" was retrieved and incorporated into the new building. Williamson chose the Jacobean Revival style for its openness. This was in part due to the Denver school board's requirement that window space equal 25 percent of the floor space.

Therefore, windows in the new high school were installed to reach the ceiling of each room. The three-story redbrick edifice was greatly enhanced with blond brick and terra-cotta trim. Above the three arched door entrances was the crowning feature of Williamson's design, a 162-foot-tall clock tower, modeled after Independence Hall in Philadelphia, Pennsylvania.

Inside, the first floor included a main lobby with gray Ozark marble and featured built-in trophy cases of curved plate glass. Greek statues adorned the lobby, the main hall, and the base of the grand staircase. Construction was completed, at a cost of nearly $2 million, in time for the 1925 fall term. The "face of an angel" carving quickly became the school's mascot, and the East High sports teams were known as the Angels.

Today the famed clock tower includes a museum full of archival information and a prominent wall featuring myriad photographs of alumni students. Among the many noted alumni are Hollywood actors Ward Bond and Don Cheadle; folk singer Judy Collins; First Lady Mamie Doud Eisenhower; Hattie McDaniel, the first African American actress to win an Academy Award, for *Gone with the Wind*; Jack Swigert, a NASA astronaut who was a member of the *Apollo 13* crew; as well as Philip Bailey, Larry Dunn, and Andrew Woolfolk, original members of the rock band Earth, Wind & Fire.

East High School is a historical landmark listed on the National Register.

Also in east Denver, George W. Clayton College was established in 1911. George W. Clayton was born in Philadelphia on February 22, 1833. Because he shared a birth date with George Washington, Clayton's parents named him George Washington Clayton, in honor of the country's first president. Clayton was one of the '59ers who arrived in Denver during the great gold rush of 1859. He opened a mercantile business in the heart of Denver's commercial district, Larimer and Fifteenth Streets. The business did so well that in 1882, he replaced the original structure with a four-story stone building he named the Clayton Building.[12]

Denver's George W. Clayton College. DENVER PUBLIC LIBRARY

Throughout the years, Clayton invested in real estate, eventually owning property in Capitol Hill, Park Hill, and University Hills. On August 15, 1889, George Washington Clayton died at his desk in the Clayton Building. The following day, the *Denver Post* printed a tribute to Clayton, extolling him as "a man who never appeared in print if he could avoid it but did anonymous acts of kindness." Following his death, the executors of his will revealed that Clayton had bequeathed the better portion of his estate, estimated at some $5 million, to found the George W. Clayton school for orphaned boys. Clayton specified that he wanted the school to be cost-free and provide above-standard care for the boys.

Twelve years later, the City and County of Denver established the **George W. Clayton Trust and College** (3801 Martin Luther King Blvd., Denver). The campus included the two-story brick school building, an administration building, and four dormitories. Designed and built by Maurice Biscoe and Henry Hewitt, the buildings had elements of the Italian Renaissance Revival style. The college even had its own powerhouse. The *Rocky Mountain News* reported the completion of the campus construction in the August 2, 1911, issue:

> *The George W. Clayton College is ready to receive orphan boys, and will be opened October 1, of this year. For ten years or more the trustees*

of the college have been preparing for this time, and a fine, modern building is ready for occupancy, with surrounding farm lands. Harry C. Kephart has been appointed general manager, and Dr. Frederick W. Bancroft, physician. A general course will be mapped out and the instructors and attendants appointed. The trustees are determined not to exceed the endowment in operating expenses. For this reason only fifty students will be received until the cost of maintenance has been determined.

Within ten years of the Pikes Peak gold rush, the Platte Valley area, approximately ten miles south of Denver, was the largest producer of wheat, barley, oats, fruits, and vegetables and provided a fair amount of the meat supply to the booming town of Denver. The area did not go unnoticed by William N. Byers, editor of the *Rocky Mountain News*. In the June 17, 1869, issue of the paper, Byers editorialized: "The Platte Valley is not surpassed in Colorado, either for variety or richness of soil, or for the extent and excellence of its improvements."

The first to arrive in the Platte Valley in 1859 was an enterprising young man with a vision. Richard S. Little was a thirty-year-old farmer and educated civil servant from Grafton, New Hampshire. In 1860 Little, employed by the Capital Hydraulic Company, conducted a survey for an irrigation ditch along the South Platte River. Surveying along the river south from Denver, Little envisioned the farming possibilities in an area where the river roamed through a low valley. By 1862 Little had made the Platte Valley his home, becoming the first permanent settler when he filed for a homestead claim. He built a log cabin near the South Platte River, just south of where Bowles Avenue and Santa Fe cross today. Here he brought his wife, Angeline, to the Colorado Territory and began a farm and raised cattle. In 1864 a meeting was held in the Littles' log cabin to organize Littleton's first school district. Lewis B. Ames was elected president; R. T. Hussy, secretary; and Richard S. Little, treasurer. For the first year, classes were held in the Littles' cabin.

In 1865 Harry Pickard donated a portion of his land, located approximately a mile north of Littleton and just east of the South Platte River, for the first school. John Bell built the one-room **Littleton Log Cabin**

Littleton's first school was a log cabin. AUTHOR'S COLLECTION

The interior of Littleton's one-room schoolhouse. AUTHOR'S COLLECTION

Schoolhouse (628 South Gallup St., Denver) at a cost of $65. The structure, measuring sixteen by seventeen feet, was covered with a sloping sod roof. Inside, rough tables and benches made of local pine provided seating and work areas for the pupils. A pine desk and chair were made for the teacher, and a box stove heated the room. The school opened in time for the fall term, enrolling fifteen students. Lewis B. Ames was the first teacher, receiving a salary of $40 a month. The next year, his wife, Laura Ames, taught the students at a salary of $50 a month.[13]

Littleton's first school served the community's education needs until 1873, when a larger school was built on Rapp Street. Today the historic log cabin school sits on the grounds of the Littleton Museum. The structure is listed with the Colorado Rural School Buildings Property listings as well as on the State Register.

Douglas County

Douglas County, established in 1861, was one of the first counties to establish a county-wide school district. Widely praised at the time for its comprehensive curriculum, the Douglas School District remains one of the best in the state.

In 1874 members of the new school board voted to purchase two lots on the corner of Cantril and Third Streets in Castle Rock, the county seat. Reporting on the event, the local newspaper wrote, in part: "Steps are being taken to put up a $3,000 schoolhouse." The following year, a two-story clapboard building was erected on the Third Street side, with barbed-wire fencing surrounding the schoolyard in an effort to keep livestock out. It was fondly referred to as the "school on school-house hill."

Ten years later, a graded curriculum that included monthly tests was introduced to the students of Douglas County. Soon the student population doubled. Rural families sent their children to the school in Castle Rock, where boarding was made available during the five-month term in local homes. Within three years the current schoolhouse could no longer accommodate the growing student population. In 1888, an addition to the school was erected on the north end for $1,500. In January 1896 the "school on school-house hill" burned down. The January 7, 1896, issue of the *Castle Rock Journal* reported the disaster:

On Wednesday morning a few minutes before 9 o'clock smoke was observed from the roof of the schoolhouse and in a few minutes the entire roof was in flames. The volunteer fire department responded quickly but it was found that the hose was not long enough to reach the building and all hopes of saving it was abandoned. All the furniture and books were taken out as well as many of the doors and windows. The disaster is a sad loss to the town of Castle Rock as the insurance which amounts to $2500 will not nearly replace the building. Then again the school, which is the most successful the district has ever had, will be seriously interfered with.

A year after the fire, a new **Castle Rock School** (Third and Cantril Streets, Castle Rock) was erected at the same location. Built of local sandstone from the Castle Rock Quarry, the two-story building sparkled with the pinkish stone color. Rectangular windows on each floor provided added interior light. Above the arched entrance, a square three-story bell tower became the crowning feature. Twelve-foot-high ceilings graced an interior floored with solid oak. Today the Castle Rock School is one of Colorado's finest examples of the Italian Villa style of architecture.

Over the years the Castle Rock school district found that while the graded curriculum, incorporated into the teaching program in 1884, was highly effective, it was also expensive for the small school district. The *Castle Rock Journal* of April 22, 1898, reported:

Castle Rock is at the present maintaining a high school course, but with considerable difficulty however. Half of the scholars in attendance come from outside of town, and their parents in addition to paying their regular taxes, have to pay tuition. A joint high school district, consisting of 30 odd districts in the county would make possible a strong institution to which all might have admission on equal grounds.

Lawmakers in Douglas County agreed. State Representative James Frank Gardner and Congressman Cole Briscoe, aided by Superintendent of Schools Frank Daniel Ball, wrote legislation that would allow counties statewide to oversee and maintain schools in their individual counties. The *Castle Rock Journal* ran an editorial endorsing the measure in the July 9, 1897, issue:

> *The birth of the Douglas County School [legislation] is an interesting chapter in Colorado history. Cole Briscoe came to Douglas County from Illinois where he witnessed a struggle by the townspeople to maintain a privately endowed college at which tuition fees precluded the attendance of poorer children in the community. Thus, with his deep friendship for Frank Ball and a great respect for his abilities, he became excited over the possibility of a county school system created by the state. It was Cole Briscoe's strenuous efforts, as a member of the House from Douglas County, that accomplished the introduction and the potential passage of the school bill in the Legislature.*

In January 1899, Congressman Cole Briscoe presented House Bill 114 to the members of the Colorado House of Representatives in Denver. In February 1900 the bill finally passed and was signed into law.

Douglas County is home to two additional historic rural schools. The **Lone Tree School** (off Tall Horse Trail, seven miles south of the Colorado Highway 105/67 junction south of Sedalia), a small, one-room clapboard schoolhouse just south of Larkspur on Colorado Highway 105, was the second school to serve students who lived along West Plum Creek. It was constructed by Newton Grout, founder of the community. The building was assessed by Colorado Preservation Inc. as one of the finest crafted buildings of its type.

Built in 1868, **Glen Grove School** (7300 Perry Park Rd., Larkspur) was the first school built in the West Plum Creek area. The one-room frame building was twelve by fifteen feet. Glen Grove School operated on what was considered a "summer school" schedule, April to August, coinciding with the farming season. In an effort to reach more students, the small schoolhouse was loaded onto a buckboard and moved to various locations throughout the West Plum Creek community. Finally, in 1876, the schoolhouse was set on land along Spring Creek. The years of moving the building around the area had taken their toll, and the

Students pose for a class photo. CARNEGIE LIBRARY FOR LOCAL HISTORY–BOULDER

weathered boards had deteriorated. According to Douglas County historian Josephine Marr, "When a bull snake crawled through the floor and slithered across the foot of Clayborne Wilson, Benjamin Quick decided it was time to build a new school."[14]

Quick donated three acres of land next to the land and sawmill business of his son-in-law, John Cantril. There, a new, slightly larger one-room frame school was built. A nearby irrigation ditch provided fresh water. The pupils took a water bucket to the ditch several times a day, and a common dipper was used by the teacher and students. A narrow path behind the schoolhouse led to the outhouse. A sign read "Ladies to the right, gents to the left." When the community conducted a fundraising event to purchase an organ for the schoolhouse, not all approved. Years later, Mrs. Nell Billings Etling, who was the teacher at that time, recalled:

Mr. Quick did not approve of the organ. When I asked him to donate for it he snorted, "Hell's Bells! No. We hired you to teach these kids the three Rs, not to sing to them." I replied, "I am teaching them the three Rs and I'm not going to sing to them but with them." After attending the entertainment—25 cents admission—he gave $10.00 toward the organ. The organ cost $40.[15]

It is quite possible that Benjamin Quick warmed to the idea of an organ when he learned the school was also going to serve as the community church on Sundays. That, and the fact that his daughter, Mrs. Clara Quick Cantril, would be teaching the Sunday school classes. Sadly, in 1887 the schoolhouse was the scene of Clara Quick Cantril's funeral.

The historic Glen Grove School still stands at Perry Park Road, north of Palmer Lake.

At the southeastern edge of Douglas County, a few miles east of the Platte-Arkansas Divide area, Joseph Franklin Gile established the small community of Spring Valley in July 1860. Local rancher George Crofutt provided the details of the early settlement in a self-published account titled *Grip-Sack Guide to Colorado*. Regarding the beginnings of Spring Valley, Crofutt wrote:

It was settled on July 10th, 1860 by Redman, Lincoln, Giles, Sheldon, Spencer and a small boy. Of these, two were killed by Indians (Redman and Lincoln,) one "skipped the county." Sheldon is happy and prosperous at Colorado City, and the "small boy" is recording events, and hunting a "grubstake."

In 1865, School District No. 3, one of the original school districts of Douglas County, was established at Spring Valley. District citizens, including John Geiger and Harrison Bucks, built the **Spring Valley School** (Spring Valley Road, Larkspur), a simple one-room clapboard building located across the road from the local post office building and Jacob Geiger's Grange store. The structure, erected atop a stone foundation, included a gabled roof supporting a redbrick chimney. The first school district directors were Sam Well, president; Joseph Franklin Gile, treasurer; and P. McCumber, secretary. Carl Mathews later recalled a school story told to him by his mother, Mary, who attended Spring Valley School in 1874: "Over two hundred Ute Indians were camped about a mile southeast of the school during the month of July. An Indian boy shot a ground squirrel on the run. Then he threw the dead gopher up to shoot more arrows into it while in the air."

Through the years the school building served a variety of purposes. In addition to such school activities as spelling bees and school plays, it also hosted political gatherings, church services, weddings, and funerals.

In March 1884, tragedy struck the Spring Valley community. Young Jennie Richie was at Geiger's Grange store when she collapsed and died. It was quickly determined that her cause of death was smallpox. The following month the Divide Grange Co-operative Association refused to do business with Geiger's Grange store. Lorenzo Leppart, a popular merchant who drove his peddler's wagon throughout the area, also contracted smallpox. Now with two confirmed victims of the disease, the local Spring Valley newspaper felt it their duty to report the potential epidemic.

> *When the disease was pronounced genuine he [Leppart] was in the Postoffice [*sic*] here, and the school children were all exposed. As soon as the fact was made known school was dismissed and precaution methods have been employed to keep the children and those who have been exposed from association with others. Intense excitement prevails in the vicinity. Leppart is Postmaster and no one goes to the office. The inconvenience necessitates the leaving of our mail matters at Greenland.*

Leppart died of smallpox on January 27, 1885. That same month, four more cases were reported. Again, the local Spring Valley newspaper alerted the community:

> *The disease is confined to one house. Those who have it are Miss Jennie Richie, who was engaged to be married to Mr. Leppart, and who went and stayed from the time he was taken sick till the time of his*

death. Mr. Jacob Geiger, Mrs. Jacob Geiger, and little girl. Mr. John Geiger has moved his family up to John Prock's out of the way of the smallpox.

Curiously, three months later the post office building and the Grange store burned down. The Spring Valley newspaper reported:

It is not known how the fire originated. Mr. Knowles, John Pollock, and Philip Crawshaw were soon on the ground, and to them we are under obligation for saving the school house [sic] *as large pieces of burning wood were blown to it from the burning buildings.*

Evidently the smallpox epidemic ended, perhaps due to the burning of the buildings. Later that year of 1885, thanks to the efforts of Jessie Knowles, a new organ was acquired and placed in the Spring Valley School. New school board members were elected, and they quickly approved a measure for improvements to the building. The *Castle Rock Journal* reported the measure in the May 20, 1885, issue:

The School election passed off quietly at this place. Jesse Knowles was elected president of the board. A tax of three mills was voted for the teacher's fund, one mill for incidental funds, and one half mill to procure maps and a globe. Our school will be well equipped with modern appliances and will be the banner school of the country.

The Spring Valley School served the community until its closure in 1946. The historic building remained empty for several years and was finally acquired by the Douglas County Historical Society. In 1974 the Historical Society sold the schoolhouse to Mr. and Mrs. Robert Beadles. The couple restored the building and converted it into their summer residence. The Beadles were instrumental in documenting the history of the schoolhouse, which led to its placement on the National Register of Historic Places. It remains a private residence on private property.

Four miles west of Sedalia in Douglas County, area residents built the **Indian Park School** (1403 Colorado Hwy. 67, Sedalia) in 1884. William Smith and his wife, Hannah, donated an acre of their farmland to the school district for a new schoolhouse. The single-story clapboard building included rectangular windows inside simple wooden frames. The steep gable roof was enhanced with overhanging eaves. The entrance was through an enclosed cloakroom. Inside, the one-room schoolhouse included new desks and a handsome slate board. Twelve students attended classes that first school term of 1884. As was common with many rural schools, the Indian Park School also served as the local community center, where families gathered for social activities, holiday parties, and dances. Indian Park School served the area for seventy-four years before closing in 1958, although the building remained in use as the community center.

In 1972 the two acres of land that included the school as well as the Indian Park Cemetery behind the schoolhouse were acquired by the Indian Park Schoolhouse Association in an effort to preserve both

The one-room clapboard Indian Park School is nestled in the foothills of the Rocky Mountains. AUTHOR'S COLLECTION

historic sites. Through their efforts, the schoolhouse was reopened and became host to many community events. Due to these preservation efforts, Indian Park School was listed on the National Register of Historic Places on February 8, 1978.

El Paso County

In 1874 Jonathan R. Kennedy founded the Colorado Institute for the Education of Mutes in Colorado Springs. It was modeled after the Kansas State School for the Deaf, where Kennedy had previously served as steward. For the first two years, the school operated in a rented house in the downtown area of the city. It is interesting to note that of the seven original students, three were Kennedy's children. His daughter Emma met and later married another student, Frank H. Chaney. Frank and Emma Chaney had a son they named Lon Chaney, who became a famous silent-era Hollywood actor.[16]

In 1876, the year Colorado achieved statehood, Kennedy spoke before the new state legislature, lobbying to establish a new school that would serve handicapped students from grades one through twelve. To convince the government leaders, Kennedy presented his three deaf children, who demonstrated their abilities to communicate through Kennedy's educational program. With government approval, the Colorado legislature appropriated $5,000 for the new school. Kennedy returned to Colorado Springs to make the expanded version of his school a reality. Colorado Springs founder William Jackson Palmer purchased thirty-five acres a mile east of town. Known as Knob Hill, the site was near the famous laboratory of Nikola Tesla. The three-story building was constructed of red brick with native sandstone accents along the second story. Completed by the fall of 1876, the new school was named the **Colorado School for the Deaf and Blind** (33 North Institute St., Colorado Springs).

Over the years more buildings were added to what would become a fabulous campus. The ten buildings were constructed of Castle Rock rhyolite and featured different styles, from Neoclassical to Collegiate Gothic.

Today the state-funded Colorado School for the Deaf and Blind continues to educate deaf and blind students. The buildings of the historic campus are listed with the Colorado Rural School Buildings Property listing, as well as on the State Register.

In 1881 the City of Colorado Springs, in conjunction with El Paso County, embarked on a ten-year plan to construct schools in the city's various communities. The final school built during the program was the **Lowell Elementary School** (831 South Nevada Ave., Colorado Springs). The building was designed and built by the Denver architectural firm of Theodore Boal and Herbert Lee. By 1910 the school had more than one thousand students, making it the largest school in the city. The Lowell Elementary School served the students of the community for eighty years before closing in 1982.

In the suburbs of Colorado Springs, the **Black Forest School** (6770 Shoup Rd., Colorado Springs) was built in 1921. It was the first public building in the Black Forest community. Children were enrolled in first through eighth grades, beginning in the fall of 1921. In addition to chil-

This log cabin schoolhouse served the children of Black Forest. HEATH GAY

dren's education, the building was also used as a church on Sundays, as a summer Bible school for children, and for community social events. In 1925 an addition was added to the front of the building for a cloakroom and a place to store coal. The log cabin rural schoolhouse was only open for twenty years, closing in 1945. The building is associated with the Rural School Buildings in Colorado as well as listed on the National Register.

Jefferson County

In 1927 the **Fruitdale Grade School** (10801 West 44th Ave., Wheat Ridge) was built in the town of Wheat Ridge. The two-story brick building was designed and built by well-known Denver architect Temple Buell. The building included several elements of the Art Deco architectural style, made popular in the 1920s. A few of the character-defining features included many double-pane windows, with detailed basket-weave brickwork separating the first- and second-story windows. Additional brickwork, in a zigzag pattern, enhanced the roofline as well as the cornice and doorway entrance. The Fruitdale Grade School not only served the education needs of the children but also became the primary gathering center for community events. In 1954 a small one-story addition was built on the west side of the building, including elements of the Prairie architectural style. The Fruitdale Grade School closed in 1978.

Larimer County

Approximately forty miles south of the Wyoming border, the small agricultural community of Bellvue was established in 1873. Located on the south side of the Cache la Poudre River, the town was named for Bellvue Dome, a landmark in the area known as Pleasant Valley. In 1879 a one-room schoolhouse was built to serve the educational needs of the children in the area. Constructed of natural stone, the **Bellvue School** (4042 North CR 25E, Bellvue) is a rare example of the few surviving stone schoolhouses in the state. Associated with the Rural School Buildings list, it is also on the National Register.

Not far from Bellvue was the small community of Stove Prairie. On April 5, 1878, settlers in the area organized their own school district.

Emanuel Vannorsdell, a father of ten, and Harlan Bosworth, a father of two, built a one-room clapboard schoolhouse. Located at the junction of Stove Prairie and Rist Canyon Roads, the building included four windows and vertical board and batten siding. The entrance was a simple plank door under a gabled roof with a bell tower. Belle Thompson was the first schoolmarm, with twenty students at the new Stove Prairie School. Because there was no water, students brought water with them to class and were also asked to bring wood for the stove. A year later the bell tower was removed and the roof sealed, as strong winter winds blew snow through the cracks and into the classroom.

By 1904 the student population was more than the schoolhouse could accommodate, and a one-room log building was constructed at the junction of Stove Prairie and Buckhorn Canyon Roads.[17]

In 1920 school enrollment had dropped drastically, with a total of three students that school term. The school closed the following year but reopened in 1928 with fifteen students. After the statewide school consolidation in 1960, **Stove Prairie School** (3891 Stove Prairie Rd., Stove Prairie) was one of very few one-room rural schoolhouses that remained open. In 1964 the school was expanded, adding a second classroom. Running water was piped into the area, and an indoor bathroom was installed.

Today, Stove Prairie School serves the small community as a social center, providing a venue for weddings, funerals, and church services.

In 1862 Congress passed the Morrill Act, which allowed a total of sixty-eight land-grant colleges to be established across the country. In 1870, a full six years before Colorado statehood, Colorado Territorial Governor Edward M. McCook received one of the proposed land grants. Governor McCook formed a twelve-member board of trustees to draft basic rules for governing the institution, as well as oversee the purchase and management of property and building construction. The institution of higher learning was first known as the Colorado Agricultural College.

In 1871 Robert Dazell deeded a thirty-acre tract of his land in Larimer County to the college board. Located just south of the town boundary of Fort Collins, the county seat, this tract of land served as the central campus. The following year, the Larimer County Land Improvement Company donated an eighty-acre tract. In 1874 the territorial legislature

An early-days school bus. DENVER PUBLIC LIBRARY

allocated $1,000 for the construction of buildings. The citizens and businesses of Fort Collins held fundraisers to acquire additional funds for the college. In the spring of 1874, the local Grange No. 6 sponsored a community picnic and "planting event" at the corner of West Laurel Street and College Avenue. Later, a group of men from the Grange plowed twenty acres of land south of the intersection. Before the year was out, the first building was erected. A 16-by-24-foot redbrick building, known as the "Claim Shanty," was the first structure to symbolize the Fort Collins college.[18]

Following Colorado statehood in August 1876, the state legislature created the State Board of Agriculture to govern the school. One of the board's first decisions was to enact a mill levy to raise money for additional buildings. Two years later, in December 1878, the cornerstone building of the campus was erected just south of College Avenue. Affectionately known as "Old Main," the doors were opened to students for the first term on September 1, 1879. That first enrollment consisted of five students. The following year, under college president Elijah Evans Edwards, enrollment grew to twenty-five students. Nearly one hundred years later, on March 5, 1968, the flagship building burned during a Vietnam War protest.

As the college progressed in student enrollment and agricultural instruction, so did expansion of the campus. Of the many buildings

One of the first buildings erected on the new agricultural college campus, later named Colorado State University. DENVER PUBLIC LIBRARY

constructed over the years, a few are included with the Colorado State Historic Preservation's Multiple Listings. An 1894 graduate of Colorado Agricultural College, Harlan Thomas, went on to be a well-respected architect. So much so that his alma mater hired him to design and build several buildings on the campus. The **Mechanical Arts Building** is the only remaining example of Thomas's work. Constructed the year after he graduated, Thomas erected the redbrick structure in the Richardsonian Romanesque style.

Spruce Hall, one of the oldest buildings on the campus, was built by Hiram Pierce in 1881. Located at the southwest corner of College Avenue and Plum Street, the building received a complete renovation in 1990.

The **Colorado Agricultural College** building was built in 1894. The simple blond-brick structure with a hipped roof housed a variety of educational departments over several decades. From 1905 to 1927 it was known as Laurel Hall and was the main library on campus.

The Botanical and Horticultural Laboratory (southwest corner of College Avenue and Laurel Street) was constructed in 1890 at a cost of $4,000. Designed by O. Bulow, the one-story Queen Anne structure was constructed atop a raised basement built of natural sandstone. The redbrick building included an inviting porched entrance. Behind the building, a small shed was constructed using salvaged bricks from the first college building, the "Claim Shanty." Four years later the laboratory was refurbished to house the Domestic Economy department.

At the southeast corner of Howes Street and Laurel Avenue, James Murdoch built the **Simon Guggenheim Hall** in 1910. The two-story brick building with elements of the Neoclassical architectural style was financed by the Guggenheim family of Philadelphia, known for their many smelting companies, including one in Leadville.

Ammons Hall has a unique history of its own. The Italian Renaissance Revival was designed and built by Eugene G. Groves in 1922. The blond-brick building featured an arcade of three arched windows on either side of the large arched entrance. Four corner pavilions completed the handsome structure. Ammons Hall was constructed to meet the needs of the growing female population on campus. It served as a women's dormitory, a gymnasium, and the Women's Social Center. Ironically, the building was not named for the first female professor, Theodosia G. Ammons; rather, it was named for her brother, Governor Elias M. Ammons.

In 1957, under President William "Bill" Morgan, the college curriculum expanded to offer doctoral degrees in several departments. Through Morgan's efforts, the Colorado General Assembly approved the elevated status of the college with the new name of Colorado State University.

Notable graduates of Colorado State University include two Colorado governors, William Ritter and Roy Romer; US Senator Wayne Allard; Olympic swimmer and gold medalist Amy Van Dyken; award-winning actor Keith Carradine; and veterinarian and cowboy poet Baxter Black.

The **Nutrition Research Laboratory** was built in 1902. The simple building with a hipped roof served as the college bathhouse until 1910, when it was refurbished and became the home of the Department of Zoology and Entomology until 1937.

The historic buildings on the **Colorado State University** (300 University Ave., Fort Collins) campus are included in the Multiple Property Listings with Colorado Preservation Inc.

The **Old Fort Collins High School** (1400 South Remington St., Fort Collins) was designed and built by William N. Bowman in 1924. The three-story redbrick building was enhanced with a three-story columned portico. The gabled roof supported a tall cupola. Inside, classrooms were on the first and second floors; a music room and an auditorium were on the third floor. Today the Old Fort Collins High School is part of the CSU campus, serving as the University Center for the Arts.

At the triangular junction of East Laurel, Mathews, and Peterson Streets, just south of downtown Fort Collins, the **Laurel School** (330 East Laurel St., Fort Collins) was erected in 1906. The two-story brick building, built by Montezuma Fuller, was a simple rectangular structure. Years later the Laurel School became Centennial High School. Today the historic Laurel School is the cornerstone of the Laurel School Historic District.

Just west of Loveland and east of Estes Park in today's Arapaho and Roosevelt National Forests, Rattlesnake Park was a settlement dating to the 1870s. In 1873 folks in the settlement felt there were enough children in the area to warrant a schoolhouse. Amas Penoyer, one of the settlement's founding fathers, offered a portion of his land for the structure. Regarding the construction, Glen Durrell offered the following quote in his article "Homesteading Colorado," published in the winter 1974 issue of *Colorado Magazine*:

> *The men set a day, brought their sod cutters, wagons, spades and carpenter tools, and went to work. In a remarkably short time the building was up, the windows and door installed. A teacher was found and the school was underway.*

Built of logs cut from the forest, the tiny log cabin school, known as the **Pinewood School** (County Road 18E/Pole Hill Rd., Rattlesnake Park), served the community for several years. The Pinewood School sits on land overlooking the southeast end of Pinewood Reservoir. It is listed among the Rural Schools of Colorado.

Alice Boardman was one of the teachers at Pinewood. Local historian Kenneth Jessen recounts the following tale:

One day there was a surprise visit by the county superintendent of schools. He found the Pinewood School deserted, but heard voices in the forest. He came across Boardman skinning a dead calf, providing her pupils with a firsthand lesson in animal anatomy. The story goes on to say that one of her students became a prominent surgeon.

In 1875 the county commissioners approved a $300 construction project to build a road through Rattlesnake Park. Known as Pole Hill Road, the road allowed easier access to both Loveland and Estes Park. Because of this, the area grew in both business and settlements. Soon a new school

The Pinewood log cabin schoolhouse. KENNETH JESSEN

was needed for the growing population. In 1904 a new and larger frame school was constructed about a quarter of a mile west of the old school. However, due to the falling agriculture economy, many folks moved away for better opportunities. By 1919 the school was no longer in use.

A few years later a new school was built from the lumber of the old school. This school was in use until 1957, when the school district was consolidated.

Just north of the Poudre River and a few miles east of Fort Collins, the Plummer School District was established on June 9, 1882. James Ezra Plummer donated a three-hundred-square-yard plot of his land to the Larimer County School District for a school building. A small one-room clapboard building originally constructed on the property was named Plummer School. In 1906 the school district contracted for a new building.

By this time, the city of Fort Collins had grown considerably and had stretched east to the edge of Plummer's farm property. The new **Plummer School** (2524 East Vine Dr., Fort Collins) was erected at the northwest corner of Timberline and Sugar Factory Roads. Noted archi-

The Plummer School in northern Colorado. KENNETH JESSEN

tect Montezuma Fuller was awarded the district's contract. Fuller incorporated elements of Romanesque and Italian Renaissance Revival styles in his design. Constructed atop a natural stone foundation, the two-story redbrick building featured an arched double-door entrance flanked by double windows on either side. Atop the flat roof a central, rectangular tower with an arcaded bell tower was erected. Complete with sandstone windowsills and capped with an elongated hipped roof, the tower housed the new school bell. Perhaps the most telling feature of the Romanesque style was Fuller's choice of Roman numerals in the large bronze plaque placed on the facade of the building, just below the belfry. The year of construction (1906) was carved with the characters "A.D. MDCCCCVI" rather than the conventional "MCMVI."

Inside, there were two classrooms, one on each floor. The upper-floor classroom featured a divider in the center of the room, which, when folded out, created two smaller rooms. The Plummer School was also used for community meetings, weddings, and funerals. After school consolidations within the various districts in 1959–1960, the historic Plummer School remained empty for several years. In 1977 the building was purchased by Steve and Kay Roy, who renovated the building and opened an antiques store.[19] The Plummer School has changed ownership over many years and remains a private property. Associated with the Rural School Buildings in Colorado List, the historic building is also listed on the National and State Registers.

Pueblo County

In the town of Pueblo, the **Pueblo Central High School** (431 East Pitkin Ave., Pueblo) was founded in 1881. The first school building was built in the south end of Pueblo in 1882. The two-story schoolhouse was constructed of local rough-faced pink rhyolite. The trim around the windows and arched entrance was of smooth cream-colored Manitou sandstone. Above the entrance was the crowning jewel—an eighty-foot-tall bell tower topped with a mansard roof. In 1886 the first graduating class consisted of nine students. Pueblo Central High School was one of the first schools in Colorado to include vocational education in its curriculum, thanks to the efforts of the superintendent of schools, Preston

Search, in 1889. By the turn of the century, the Central High School facility could no longer accommodate the increase in student enrollment. When the new facility was completed in 1906, the old Central High School, or "Stone Schoolhouse," as it was fondly called, served as an elementary school.

In 1979 the building was saved from demolition by Pueblo's citizens. After a massive renovation effort, the historic schoolhouse reopened as the Pueblo Ballet Company.

In 1905 respected Denver architect Robert Roeschlaub was hired to design and build a new school complex. A groundbreaking ceremony took place in 1906. Roeschlaub's grand design encompassed the entire block of Grant Avenue on the north and Orman Avenue on the south, between Broadway and Michigan Streets. The construction project would last six years. Built in the Beaux Arts Neoclassical style, the blond-brick building was four stories tall and included a raised basement. Five fluted Ionic columns graced the center entrance of the school. Extended wings with triple windows enhanced the edifice on either side of the entrance. When the building was completed in late 1906, Roeschlaub moved on to construct the gymnasium building, which included a large meeting room for the administration and two other outlying structures.

Pueblo's second **Central High School** (216 East Orman Ave., Pueblo) is the only high school to have graduated two Medal of Honor recipients: William J. Crawford, 1936, and Carl L. Sitter, 1940. Other notable high school graduates include Robert M. Stillman, US Air Force general; Walter W. Johnson, governor of Colorado for one term in 1950; and comedian Dan Rowan, of the hit television show *Rowan & Martin's Laugh-In*.

Today the Central High School continues to serve the educational needs of Pueblo's high school students.

Also in Pueblo is the historic **Edison School** (900 West Mesa St., Pueblo), located in an educational complex composed of six buildings. Construction began in 1909. The building was designed by Dr. Richard W. Corwin, a Pueblo school board member. The central building was a one-story structure built of blond-colored brick with elements of the Italianate style. However, Corwin's design deviated from classic Italianate style by placing windows near the ceiling on three sides of the classrooms in an effort to provide uniform, diffused light and improved ventilation. Later, two one-room buildings were added on either side of the building as "unit schoolhouses."

Two additional units as well as a four-room schoolhouse were erected in 1923. Dr. Corwin remained on the Pueblo school board for forty-four years.

Approximately twenty-five miles south of Pueblo lie the aged remains of the Doyle Settlement. The one-room schoolhouse, Colorado's oldest school building, stands vigil overlooking the Huerfano River.

The Doyle Settlement was the work of Joseph Bainbridge Lafayette Doyle in 1859. Born in 1817 in Shenandoah, Virginia, Doyle came west as a young man and became a trapper and trader for William Bent at Bent's Fort in 1839. He was one of the builders of the fort known as El Pueblo, near the current city of Pueblo. He then became a territorial lawyer and a farmer, which led him to the Huerfano River area. Doyle

The Doyle Schoolhouse is Colorado's oldest school. HEATH GAY

purchased twelve hundred acres of land along two miles of the Huerfano River from the Vigil and St. Vrain Land Grant. Here, he established his wife, Maria, and their children, building a large ranch house he called "Casa Blanca" with lumber shipped from St. Louis. Doyle and his hired help cultivated more than six hundred acres of land for crops, built irrigation ditches, and established one of the first flour mills in Colorado. In this capacity, Doyle became a pioneer agriculturalist, and the Doyle Settlement was the site of one of the earliest agricultural communities in Colorado. A community of Doyle's workers soon grew into a small settlement. Structures began to be built on the site in 1859.

Doyle established a school, where the workers' children attended classes with his own children. Located southeast of Pueblo along the Huerfano River, **Doyle Schoolhouse** (on Doyle Road, nineteen miles southeast of US Highway 50, Pueblo) is a one-room schoolhouse built of adobe and wood siding. Wooden shingles protected the A-frame roof. Doyle brought in Owen J. Goldrick to teach the children. Goldrick

Owen J. Goldrick helped open Colorado's first school at the Doyle Settlement. He was Denver's first schoolteacher and founded the Denver School District. DENVER PUBLIC LIBRARY

became the state's first schoolteacher and went on to teach in Denver City, the first teacher in that new settlement as well. On Sundays the school served as a church.

Doyle was elected to the Territory Council in 1864, working toward statehood. He was elected commissioner of Huerfano County and to the State Council, as the State Senate was then called, representing Huerfano, Pueblo, and Fremont Counties. Doyle also operated a post office from his home, Casa Blanca, having been appointed postmaster. On March 4, 1864, the forty-six-year-old Doyle died of a heart attack while serving his term in Denver. Governor John Evans led the party of dignitaries escorting Doyle's wagon hearse out of Denver. At the time of his death, Doyle was one of the first millionaires in Colorado Territory. He was buried in the family cemetery on a hill not far from the school.

The **Doyle Settlement** was recognized as one of the most Endangered Historic Sites in Colorado by Colorado Preservation, Inc., at their annual "Saving Places—The Power of Place" conference on February 1, 2018. Today the entire Doyle Settlement site, including the school, is on the National Register of Historic Places and is also listed on the Colorado Register of Historic Sites.

Notes

1. Archives of Denver University.
2. Ibid.
3. Van Wyke, *The Town of South Denver*, 94.
4. "History of South High School," Denver Public Schools archives.
5. Ibid.
6. Smiley, *History of Denver*, 740.
7. Vervalin, "West Denver," 9–10.
8. Catlett, "The Story of Southwest Denver," 29.
9. Ross, *North, South, East, West—Denver's Iconic Public High Schools*. DPL
10. For a comprehensive look at Denver's early public school system, see Smiley, *History of Denver*, 740–47.
11. Ross, *North, South, East, West—Denver's Iconic Public High Schools*. DPL
12. The Clayton Building would later become the cornerstone of Larimer Square, Denver's first designated historic district.
13. Archives of the Littleton Museum. The author is a native of Littleton and attended Littleton Public Schools.
14. Marr, "Douglas County: A Historical Journey," 146.
15. Ibid., 201.

16. *Douglas County News*, "Pioneer Stories," November 4, 1965.
17. Thomas, "The History and Architecture of Poudre School District R-1."
18. Hansen, "Democracy's College in the Centennial State," 25.
19. Thomas, "The History and Architecture of Poudre School District R-1."

Chapter Six

Frontier Teacher Rachel Bassette Noel

Rachel Bassette Noel spent her adult life as a strong advocate for better education. After several years as a Denver Public Schools board member, Noel worked on desegregating Denver's schools. Because of her dedication, in 1965 Noel became the first African American elected to public office in the state of Colorado.

Rachel Bassette was born on January 15, 1918, in Hampton, Virginia. This was also the birth date of Dr. Martin Luther King Jr., whom

Rachel B. Noel was a beloved Denver school teacher who broke many barriers.
DENVER PUBLIC LIBRARY

she would later meet. Education was important to Rachel's parents, both of whom were college graduates. In 1938, at the age of twenty, Rachel graduated magna cum laude with a bachelor's degree in education from Hampton University and went on to earn a master's degree in sociology from Fisk University, both historically Black institutions of higher learning. After graduation, Rachel moved to Washington, DC. Her first job was at Southeast House, a settlement house for minority children.

During World War II, Rachel Bassette married Dr. Edmund F. Noel, himself a graduate of Fisk University. After the war, on November 30, 1949, the couple moved to Denver. In January 1950 Dr. Noel opened a medical practice at the corner of Twenty-sixth and Welton Streets in the Five Points community. Dr. Noel was also able to practice medicine at Denver's newly founded Rose Hospital. The Jewish medical facility was the only hospital in Denver at the time that allowed minority physicians to practice.

Because of the obvious lack of equal opportunities for African Americans in Denver, Rachel Bassette Noel became active in civic affairs and, later, in politics. Noel volunteered with the Parent-Teacher Association (PTA) when her two children, Edmond "Buddy" and Angela, entered the Denver Public School system. In 1963 the Denver Classroom Teacher's Association presented Noel with the Eddy Award for her dedicated service in education. In 1965 Noel boldly announced her candidacy for a six-year term on the Denver school board. With heavy support of the African American community, Noel was elected to the school board, becoming the first African American, not to mention Black female, to ever be elected to public office in Colorado. It was during her first term that Noel had the opportunity to meet Dr. Martin Luther King Jr. Inspired by his dedication to improving the lives of African Americans, Noel set about to effect change in Denver. On April 25, 1968, she presented a comprehensive plan to the school board that would provide, through integration, an equal opportunity for education to all children. Unfortunately, her plan was met with angry opposition as well as racial comments. Years later, Noel reflected on that moment:

I was calmer than I have ever been. I felt this was so important that the opportunity should not be missed. I knew I had support from my community and from many Whites too. All those years, so little had been done. In those times, there was a feeling of high morality across the country, about consideration of Black people and all the wrongs against our schools and our children—our future adults.[1]

Noel's bold plan, later known as the "Noel Resolution," eventually received school board approval on May 16, 1968. However, due to outrage and hate mail, the resolution was stalled. A year later, with new members of the school board in opposition, the desegregation measure was overturned. With the internal battle of the Denver school board over the issue growing heated, a lawsuit was filed. US District Court Judge William E. Doyle not only reinstated the desegregation measure but also broadened the scope of Noel's original plan.

However, in February 1970, thirty buses were dynamited at the Denver Public School Service Center, an act of opposition to the integration busing policy imposed by the US district court. Years later, Noel commented:

Everyone associates me with busing. I never spoke about busing. It's a mode of transportation, that's all. My stand was for equal education opportunity for all children, not for minorities to be in a segregated, afterthought status but to have all the rights and privileges. If it took a bus to do it, then so be it.[2]

Noel continued her advocacy for civil rights by volunteering with various organizations and serving on many boards. Among those were the Denver Housing Authority, the Metro Denver Urban Coalition, the Colorado Advisory Committee, and the US Civil Rights Commission.

In 1970 Noel became an assistant professor of sociology at Denver's Metro State College. In 1972 she received the Malcolm Glenn Wyer Award for her service to education. On September 27, 1976, Governor Richard Lamm appointed Noel to fill the vacancy of a CU regent's six-year term, making her the first African American regent at the University of Colorado. In 1978 Noel ran for a second term as CU regent in a statewide election; she won and served as chair for one year.

Over the next twenty years, more accolades and honors were bestowed upon Rachel Noel. In 1981 she received the honor of Distinguished Professorship at Metropolitan State College. In 1990 she received the Martin Luther King Jr. Humanitarian Award. In 1993 the University of Denver awarded her an honorary doctorate of public service. That same year, her church, the A.M.E. Church in North Denver, dedicated a stained-glass window in her honor. In 1996 Noel was inducted into the Colorado Women's Hall of Fame. On February 4, 2008, Rachel Bassette Noel died at her daughter's home in Oakland, California. She was ninety years old. A Denver middle school was renamed the **Rachel B. Noel School** in her honor.

Notes

1. Varnell, *Women of Consequence*, 194.
2. Ibid., 195.

Chapter Seven

Ring-Around-the-Rosy, a Pocket Full of Posies

Rules for Schoolchildren

Rules for Teachers—1872

1. Teachers each day will fill lamps, clean chimneys.
2. Each teacher will bring a bucket of water and a scuttle of coal for the day's session.
3. Make your pencils carefully. You may whittle nibs to the individual taste of the pupils.
4. Men teachers may take one evening each week for courtship purposes, or two evenings a week if they go to church regularly.
5. After ten hours in school, the teachers may spend the remaining time reading the Bible or other good books.
6. Women teachers who marry or engage in unseemly conduct will be dismissed.
7. Every teacher should lay aside from each pay a goodly sum of his earnings for his benefit during his declining years so that he will not become a burden on society.

8. Any teacher who smokes, uses liquor in any form, frequents pool or public halls, or gets shaved in a barber shop will give good reason to suspect his worth, intention, integrity, and honesty.

9. The teacher who performs his labors faithfully and without fault for five years will be given an increase of twenty-five cents per week in his pay, providing the Board of Education approves.

Guidelines for Student Examinations—1886

Tuesday—Penmanship, Reading, Spelling, and Algebra
Wednesday—Geography, History, Etymology, and C. Arithmetic
Thursday—Grammar, Physiology, A. and B. Arithmetic

The examinations on Thursday will be oral, and will be conducted by the superintendent of schools.

The examination will cover the whole book of Physiology, and all the Diagramming [*sic*] and Etymology of Grammar, and in Arithmetic will include Involation, Square Root and Cube Root, Arithmetical and Geometrical Progressions, the Metric Systems, Mensurations, and one hundred promiscuous examples.

All parents and those interested are cordially invited to attend.

Few smiling faces in this classroom. CARNEGIE LIBRARY FOR LOCAL HISTORY–BOULDER

Here We Go Round the Mulberry Bush: A Short History of Playgrounds

For those children lucky enough to attend public school in the nineteenth century, being inside a schoolhouse all day was no easy task. Teachers learned early on that children needed a break and needed to be outside in the schoolyard, in the fresh air and sunshine.

In those early days children played ball games, running games, tag games, and the like. It wasn't until the 1880s that playgrounds began to appear in schoolyards across the country. The concept originated in Germany and was known as "sand gardens." The idea was to provide supervised "exercise programs," as well as good health and socialization skills.

Playground equipment, if the particular school district could afford it, included metal or wooden swing sets, seesaws or teeter-totters, climbing apparatuses, and metal slides. By the late nineteenth century, the "modern Playground" concept appeared in schoolyards primarily in urban settings. Because space was limited, the giant stride (a swing on chains), maypole, and jungle gyms or monkey bars were used. Rural schools began implementing organized games supervised by the teacher, such as leapfrog, red rover, and follow-the-leader.

Playtime in the fresh air. PARK COUNTY HISTORICAL SOCIETY

America's schoolchildren did not enjoy recreation and playtime in an outdoor playground until 1886, when the first playgrounds were opened in San Francisco, California, and Boston, Massachusetts. At that time teachers and administrators began to believe that outdoor recreation provided exercise and relieved tension. Playgrounds were not free-form in those early years. Trained instructors were hired to teach children outdoor lessons and organize their play.

Soon, manufacturing companies found new business in playground apparatuses. Variations of the playground theme could be found throughout cities and in rural areas, often dictated by space and the individual community's needs and finances.

Early apparatuses were built with galvanized steel, with both vertical and horizontal elements such as ladders and chains, evidenced in the popular giant stride swinging device.

Early playground equipment. DENVER PUBLIC LIBRARY

The incorporation of playground equipment was slow and evolved over time.

1880s–1890s: Sand gardens or sandboxes were implemented.

1900s–1920s: The beginning of model playgrounds. Apparatuses such as merry-go-rounds, swing sets, and metal swinging devices called giant strides were added.

1930s: Metal slides and metal jungle gyms and seesaws became the rage.

1950s: Sports were added, including tetherball and basketball courts.

1960s: Although the playground remained, much of the equipment now was made of plastic for safety reasons.

Merry-go-rounds were always a playground favorite. HEATH GAY

Thanks to the Playground Association of America, as the playground concept caught on and the need for exercise was recognized, some companies built playgrounds for their employees. Eventually, playground equipment was replaced by newer designs and apparatuses. Materials for playground construction changed to include earthen materials, concrete, wood, and plastics. However, with the onset of the Great Depression, followed by the outbreak of World War II, the work of the PAA came to a grinding halt.

In 1933 President Franklin D. Roosevelt created the Works Progress Administration (WPA), which allowed for several federal assistance programs to put unemployed citizens back to work. Among the many projects were schools and new playgrounds. During World War II, as steel was needed for the war effort, children were encouraged to get involved in dismantling old playground equipment and gathering the material into piles for military trucks to pick up.

In 1950 *McCall's* magazine sponsored a new playground concept known as the "adventure playground." The playground equipment used had plastic end caps and corners for safety. Later, plastic and rubber would be used in making all playground equipment.

Although today's playgrounds do not contain the same equipment many of us remember from our schoolyard, it remains part of the schoolyard memories we all treasure.

Jack and Jill Went Up the Hill: Schoolyard Games

Schoolyard games not only provided a bit of exercise and a break from schoolwork but were also part of the learning process. Many of the games taught cooperation, concentration, and fairness. Traditional games included:

- **Marbles:** There are several varieties of marble games, and every schoolyard had its own version. Clay marbles were the standard until the Civil War era. Glass marbles were handmade until the turn of the twentieth century, when they began to be mass-produced by machines.

- **Jacks:** The concept of this centuries-old game is to toss the jacks, bounce a small ball, and pick up an increasing number of jacks with one hand before the ball hits the ground. Before jacks were mass-produced rocks were used and the game was called knucklebones.
- **Red rover:** Every child in America knows the schoolyard chant. One theory on the origin of this game was that it was a taunt by American children directed at the British Army. Another suggests it was named for an 1828 steamboat that ferried passengers back and forth across the river.
- **Kickball:** The game was invented in Cincinnati, Ohio, in 1917. Because of its organizational theme, it quickly became an indoor sport in gym classes across the country.
- **Jump rope:** A game for individuals or groups; there were several variations to this athletic game.

Schoolyard games. DENVER PUBLIC LIBRARY

The Rocky Mountains & Western Slope

Chapter Eight

She'll Be Comin' Round the Mountain When She Comes

Counties North of Interstate 70

Boulder County

One of the original counties formed by the Colorado Territorial Legislature in 1861, Boulder County encompassed an area from the eastern plains west to Longs Peak and the Continental Divide. At Allenspark, a small community at the foot of Longs Peak, the **Bunce School** (approximately four miles south of Allenspark, on Colorado Highway 7) was erected in 1888. The schoolhouse was built by J. H. Bunce and V. H. Rowley with broadaxe-hewn logs that were square-notched at the corners. The windows and door were simple in structure. The Bunce School served the education needs of the community until 1940. During the war years, the building became the community center.

In the western portion of Boulder County, the mining town of Salina was established in 1859 by gold miners from Salina, Kansas. In 1875 the community built a one-room frame schoolhouse on Gold Run Road. The protruded entrance featured a small round window above. The **Salina School** (536 Gold Run Rd., Salina) is believed to be the oldest schoolhouse in the county and is listed with the Metal Mining and Tourist Era Resources of Boulder County as well as on the National Register.

In 1898 the citizens of Ward, a small mining community, erected the **Ward School** (66 Columbia St., Ward). The clapboard building with

An early-days class photo at the Salina School. CARNEGIE LIBRARY FOR LOCAL HISTORY–BOULDER

a protruded entrance included three rectangular windows. The historic building now serves the community as the Town Hall.

The town of Boulder, county seat of Boulder County, is rich in educational history. The county's first high school, **Highland School** (885 Arapahoe Ave., Boulder), was completed in 1891 by the architectural firm of Varian and Sterner. Both Gothic and Romanesque styles were evident in the two-story redbrick building. The arched entrance and windows were enhanced with natural sandstone. A 1923 addition was connected to the original building by a central bay.

In 1892 Boulder's first private educational facility, **Mount St. Gertrude Academy (**970 Aurora St., Boulder), was built on University Hill. Architects Alexander Cazin and George H. Williamson designed the building in the Richardsonian Romanesque style. The first floor of the four-story structure was built of local sandstone; the upper three floors were built of brick with sandstone trim. A steep-sloping mansard roof was enhanced with a molded cornice on all sides of the structure. The main entrance was framed by a stone arch, which supported a three-story

The imposing Highland School in Boulder. CARNEGIE LIBRARY FOR LOCAL HISTORY–BOULDER

tower. Connected to the building was a single-story heating plant and laundry facility.

Inside, a central hall on the first floor ran the full length of the building, with offices and classrooms on either side. A grand staircase at the east end led to the upper floors.

When Colorado was granted statehood on August 1, 1876, the state constitution included a curious amendment: funding for a state university. This amendment aided in establishing the University of Colorado. Several cities were in contention for the school. However, with its proximity to the state capital in Denver, and its backdrop of the Flatirons against the Rockies, Boulder won the honor. With matching state funds, Boulderite David Nichols secured $15,000 from Boulder residents. Two prominent founding fathers, Anthony Arnett and Capt. Clinton Tyler, each donated sections of their landholdings for the site of the university. The site was located on a hill south of Boulder, and irrigation ditches watered the trees and, later, the landscaping.

On September 5, 1876, a month after Colorado was admitted to the Union, a bricklaying ceremony was held at the construction site of the first building. When completed, the red sandstone building stood four stories tall, including the mansard-roofed tower. A commanding structure at the base of the Flatirons to the west, it was fittingly dubbed "Old Main." This first structure would form the nucleus of the university campus.

The doors of the new **University of Colorado** (off Broadway, Colorado Highway 93, Boulder) opened on September 5, 1877. Enrollment for that first year consisted of fifteen students. That same year, the university added a preparatory school at the campus to prepare high school students for enrollment in higher education. Fifty students were enrolled at that institution during its first year. In the ensuing years, more buildings were added to the beautiful campus. The architecture style of the CU campus was a type of Italian rural architecture found in the northern

Known as "Old Main," this was the first building on the campus of the University of Colorado at Boulder. CARNEGIE LIBRARY FOR LOCAL HISTORY–BOULDER

mountains of Italy. The wonderful blend of locally quarried stone from nearby Lyons created a harmonious setting against the Flatirons. Characteristic of this style are the roughly textured red sandstone walls topped by the multilevel sloping red-tiled roofs.

Developed over twenty years, the Tuscan Vernacular Revival style, originated by Pennsylvanian architect Charles Z. Klauder, was used in all additions or expansions. This roof design was unique to the university set at the base of the Rocky Mountains.

Among those buildings, the President's House was built in 1884. F. A. Hale designed and built the Woodbury Arts and Sciences building in 1890. The Ekeley Chemical Laboratory, designed by Klauder, was a three-story brick building with Indian limestone accents. In 1918 the university's board of regents hired Klauder to become the primary architect for the university campus. In keeping with his original design, Klauder laid out a parklike landscape at the center of the campus, near "Old Main." His buildings, including Sewall Hall, named for the first university president and built in 1937, and the Norlin Library, built in 1939, were constructed primarily of pink rhyolite from the nearby Lyons quarry. A marble plaque over the doorway read "Enter here the timeless fellowship of the human spirit."

In 1908 US Senator Simon Guggenheim paid for construction of the university's first law school building. The Guggenheim Law School featured classical Greek columns. The following year, 1909, the architectural firm of Gove and Walsh was hired to build a power plant and an auditorium on campus. While the power plant, constructed in Klauder's universal design, was completed within a year, the auditorium would not be completed for nearly thirteen years. The auditorium was located at University Avenue and Seventeenth Street, the northern edge of the campus. The large red sandstone building featured octagonal corner towers in the Neo-Gothic Revival style. This was the only departure from Klauder's Tuscan Vernacular Revival design. The roof of the auditorium was red tile, conforming to the overall aesthetic of the other buildings. The interior featured custom carpeting for sound quality and plenty of seating with a good view of the stage. The auditorium was named Macky Auditorium in honor of Andrew J. Macky, president of the First National

Bank. Macky had donated $300,000 to the university for construction of the auditorium.

Unfortunately, a year into the construction of the building, Macky died. Because Andrew J. Macky's will left nothing to his adopted daughter, May Macky, she sued CU for the money her father had donated to the university. Construction was immediately halted. After nearly thirteen years of litigation, the university prevailed and the Macky Auditorium was finally completed.[1]

In 1947 Governor Lee Knous issued a proclamation creating a memorial to Colorado's military on the university campus. After years of fundraising, the three-story rectangular building opened in October 1953, with CU president Robert Stearns presiding over the ribbon-cutting ceremony. Landscaping around the University Memorial Center building included the magnificent UMC Fountain Court. The grand Glenn Miller Ballroom was named for the former CU student and captain of the Army Specialist Corps during World War II. The UMC building included a cafeteria that would later be known as the Alferd Packer Grill.

In 1936 Dr. George F. Reynolds, an internationally known Elizabethan theater scholar and CU professor, was instrumental in creating the Mary Rippon Outdoor Theatre. Noted university alumni include two Supreme Court justices, Wiley Rutledge and Byron White. The Norlin Quadrangle Historic District comprises all the historic buildings on the University of Colorado Boulder campus that have historic recognition.

Clear Creek County

The mining town of Dumont, established in 1861, was known as Mill City for its location in the Mill Creek Valley of Clear Creek County. In 1909 the community came together to build the **Dumont School** (150 CR 260, Dumont). The large two-story building was constructed in the Italian Renaissance style using local sandstone. A belfry was centered atop the schoolhouse roof. Concrete steps led to a porched entrance. A large outhouse, built of matching, blond-colored sandstone, was constructed behind the school building. There were two entrances, separated by a brick wall and labeled "Boys" and "Girls."

The Dumont School is closed but not abandoned. KENNETH JESSEN

Inside, a door off the long cloakroom led to the single classroom. The large room contained desks for the students that faced the elevated semicircular stage. This served as the teacher's space as well as a platform for school plays and various student events.

The playground on the school property included a swing set, cross bars, and a giant stride, all of which remain today. The Dumont schoolhouse served the education needs of the town for fifty years before closing in 1959. The Dumont School is on the Colorado Rural School Buildings Property list as well as the State Register and National Register.

In 1874 the citizens of the rich silver mining town of Georgetown erected the **Georgetown Public School** (809 Taos St., Georgetown). Located on the corner of Sixth and Taos Streets, the two-story brick building became the pride of Georgetown residents. Romanesque features including large double windows graced the first and second floors. Single windows were installed on both the east and west sides of each floor. The otherwise simple roof supported an open bell tower. The arched entrance door at the center of the building was enhanced by a central roof gable. Above the doorway, a rounded pediment carved into stone and

Very few school outhouses were made of brick like this one at the Dumont School. KENNETH JESSEN

placed within the brickwork read "Public School 1874." Inside, seven large classrooms accommodated more than four hundred students. The Georgetown Public School served the education needs of young scholars until 1938.

In 1939 the building was purchased by a private individual, who operated his machine repair shop out of the historic structure. During this time a portion of one side of the building was demolished in order to provide a drive-in entry for trucks.[2] In 1946 the building was acquired by another private individual, with the intent to convert the building into a mining museum. However, plans never materialized, and the historic structure sat vacant for the next sixty years. In 2006 the historic landmark school building was placed on the Endangered Places Program list by Colorado Preservation Inc. In the listing, the ominous threat was termed "Demolition by Neglect—Vacant."[3] Shortly after its listing, the Georgetown Trust for Conservation & Preservation was able to acquire the building through funds from individual donations as well as grants from the Colorado Historical Society. Executive director of the Georgetown Trust for Conservation & Preservation Cynthia Neeley said:

> *I've been at this for forty-five years. It's what I do. This building sat. It was in private hands. It was beaten up. It was not taken care of and was in terrible shape. Every decade we would try to figure out how to convince them [the owners] to sell to us.*[4]

One of Georgetown's first brick schools was made possible by the silver boom.
DENVER PUBLIC LIBRARY

In 2007 a three-phase restoration process began. It would prove to be a long process. Neeley commented on the beginning of the project:

> *Four days after we gained possession of the building, we found crystallized dynamite in the basement. Old buildings can have lots of really weird things in them. It could have blown the place up. We had already found all kinds of dynamite caps in the school. I mean*

the Gilpin County Bomb Squad were becoming my best friends. It proved to be a fascinating exercise. I didn't think we would ever get the towers back. That was a donation of a single person. The State Historical Society would help. They helped hugely with the building, but they weren't going to do the towers.[5]

Restoration experts from the firms of Hoehn Architects, Building Restoration Specialties, Long Hoeft Architects, and Silver Plume Home Services provided their services. The painstaking reconstruction of the exterior took place over the next several years. Historic photos of the interior aided the restoration inside the school building. After seven years the restoration of the Georgetown Public School was completed at a cost of just under $3 million.

In the fall of 2015, the former Georgetown Public School reopened to the public as the Georgetown Heritage Center.

The first schoolhouse in the mining town of Silver Plume was erected in 1892. Unfortunately, fire destroyed the school in 1893. Despite the economic depression caused by repeal of the Sherman Silver Purchase

The Georgetown Public School today. AUTHOR'S COLLECTION

Even the small mining town of Silver Plume could afford a brick school. AUTHOR'S COLLECTION

Act, which had backed silver, that same year the local school board commissioned Denver architect William Quayle to design and build a new school in the mining town. Construction of the new **Silver Plume School** (315 Main St., Silver Plume) began in July 1894. The two-story brick building, with several Romanesque features, was said to be the finest in the county. The structure was completed in time for the fall school term of 1895. The main floor contained two large classrooms as well as the principal's office. Two additional classrooms were on the second floor. The school board hired eight teachers for the two hundred students attending classes that year. Grades one through twelve were held in the four classrooms. For the next sixty-five years, three generations of Silver Plume citizens received their education within the halls of the Silver Plume schoolhouse. The last school term was held in 1959, with a total of twenty children. The following year a group of citizens resurrected the empty building, eventually turning it into the George Rowe Museum, named for one of the town's leading citizens.[6]

The mountain communities of Georgetown and Silver Plume are within the Georgetown and Silver Plume National Historic Landmark

District, as well as on the Colorado State List of Historic Properties. (***Note:*** All historic buildings fall under the same county registration number.)

Gilpin County

Ten years after the discovery of gold at Gregory's Diggings in 1860, the citizens of the mountain mining town of Central City finally got a schoolhouse. The first school opened in October 1862. Classes were held in a single room at Lawrence Hall, with just over 150 students in attendance that first year.[7] In 1868 classes were held at the local bowling alley, on the present site of the Teller House on Lawrence Street.[8] As this was an effort to reorganize the state school system, a separate school was established for Black children. However, due to low enrollment, the school closed. The parents of the five Black children attempted to enroll their children in the only school in town. The principal denied their enrollment. The parents hired Central City's esteemed mining attorney, Henry M. Teller, to fight for their civil rights. Teller argued that the passage of Civil Rights Act of 1866 guaranteed his clients' children the right to attend public schools. Teller further admonished the school principal for his actions, warning that if the children were not admitted to the school, he would file a lawsuit against the school, seeking damages. The principal relented and the children were admitted.

In 1869 Central City citizens voted overwhelmingly in favor of a bond issue to fund the construction of a new school. Newton D. Owen was hired to design and build the structure. Located high on High Street, aptly named for its location above the town, construction began that summer. The *Central City Register* printed the following report in its June 24, 1869, issue:

> *Mssrs. Mullin & Joblin are putting up a very substantial and permanent wall in front of the school lot. At one corner it will be sixteen feet high, and the walls are the most massive and best laid of everything in this line in Colorado. They are, in some particulars, doing the work better than the contract called for. There will never be any danger of its falling down.*

The wall was indeed massive. With the help of Cornish miners, the wall was masterfully constructed of native stone, helping to level and stabilize the hillside. Following completion of the retaining wall a month later, construction of the school stopped. The *Central City Register* explained the dilemma in the July 31, 1869, issue:

> *An inquiry is made concerning the proposed new schoolhouse. The lot is graded and the wall built in front at a total cost of near three thousand dollars, the work being let to the lowest bidder, but here it rests. No one has yet been found to take our bonds, and consequently there are no funds on hand with which to build.*

It seems as if a war of words between the editors of the town's two newspapers had erupted over the construction of the community's first school building. The September 22, 1869, issue of the *Central City Register* ran an editorial in response to an article in the *Central City Herald* that was critical of the halt in construction.

> *The* Herald *attacks our school accommodations very severely and with a good deal of justice, but we believe it is unfair to the School Board, which is at present composed of Richard Harvey, Willard Teller, and myself, D. C. Collier. The School Board has very little power. It cannot build a schoolhouse and has no authority to raise funds. All they have the authority to do is to employ teachers. This they have done. The money of the city has not been squandered by the School Board. We want a new schoolhouse more than we need new churches or hotels, and we wish every citizen of Central would hereafter refuse to give a cent toward the support of churches or benevolent objects till the needed school building is erected. We do believe that we are wanting in public spirit, or we should have one already. It is a disgrace to us as a people that we have no better quarters. Cannot something be done.*

D. C. Collier, editor of the *Central City Register* as well as a member of the school board, had information regarding the school project that he held back. The next day he revealed that new information in an advertisement in the *Central City Register*:

> *To Contractors and Builders—Bids will be received till Saturday at 4 o'clock p.m. for stone or brick work for the public school house. Brick work to be estimated by the thousand, stone by the perch. For the stone work bids must state the price of rubble work, with hammer dressed corners and openings, and for whole face hammer dressed. Payment to be estimated in cash, and also in city bonds at ninety-five cents on the face, and bearing interest at fifteen percent per annum. Propositions can be left at Richards & Crane's, or at this office.*

Two weeks later, on October 12, the *Central City Register* reported that a contract had been achieved by the school board and M. H. Root, a respected local contractor. Root took over the construction of the two-story school building, incorporating the Romanesque architectural style, popular with school buildings in the 1870s. Using native stone, the building included arched windows and doors and a low hipped roof with overhanging eaves. Inside, four classrooms, two on each floor, were furnished with new desks and various teaching materials. The wide hardwood staircase led to the second floor, where a school auditorium was built complete with a raised stage. The **Gilpin County School** (228 East 1st High St., Central City), or "Stone School," as it came to be called, was completed in September 1870. The total cost was $25,000. The new schoolhouse opened its doors on October 24. The following day, the *Central City Register* reported on the long-awaited event. The detailed account must have been written by the paper's editor, D. C. Collier, who, as previously noted, was also a member of the school board.

> *The public school of Central City was opened yesterday. Two hundred and thirteen scholars were present the first day. There are now seats for only five more scholars. Other seats will be put in to seat 60 in each of the four rooms if required, but they are not now on hand. These 213 scholars are classified in four departments and are under the charge of four teachers as follows: Mr. H. M. Hale, Principal*

and in particular charge of the first room; Miss Jennie E. Bartlett, in charge of the second room or first intermediate; Miss Mary Kirtley, in charge of the third room or second intermediate; and Miss Carrie E. Simms, in charge of the fourth room or Primary Department. The school starts off very encouragingly. It is evident that we are to have a better school than ever before in Central, because we for the first time have the means of making a good school. The new schoolhouse is an honor to the city. In size it is 66 × 40 feet on the ground and two stories in height. The grading of the lots and the building of the high bank wall were done a year ago last summer. The contract for putting up the walls, which are of stone, was let to M. H. Root last fall. Cold weather coming on, work was suspended until the past summer. The carpenter and joiner work was done by Messrs. Critchet & Owens, the plastering by Messrs. Hanus & Paul, and the painting and graining by Messrs. Glendinen & Brewer. As all the work has been done, it is not necessary of it more particularly. The carpentry work [is] good and not without elegance, especially in the large hall, the wainscoting and other wood work in the rooms nicely oaked grained, and the walls are hard finished and white as snow. The roof is covered with felt, asphaltum and gravel and surmounted with a neat belfry containing a four-hundred-pound composition bell. The four rooms are of equal size being 25 × 36. Arrangements are made for their perfect ventilation, and the light is excellent. There are in the four rooms 140 square yards of blackboard, made by applying liquid slating to the hard finished walls. The furniture is from the celebrated manufacturers, Sherwoods of Chicago. Nothing has been forgotten that would add to the elegance or comfort of the rooms. The halls which extend through the building and are eleven ft. in width, are amply supplied with books, while in the one above is an apartment designed to furnish a place for storing the globes and other school apparatus with which the school is well supplied. Taken altogether we are very proud of our new schoolhouse, and of our corps of teachers.

The Gilpin County School served the area until 1969, when a new school was built in the county. When the "Old Stone School" suffered damage from a broken boiler, the county condemned the building. Members of the Gilpin County Historical Society took over the building, made the necessary repairs, and opened the Gilpin County Historical Museum. The first Gilpin County school is listed with the Central City–Black Hawk Historic District and recognized as a National Historic Landmark.

At Thorn Lake, a small mining camp north of Central City, the **Thorn Lake Schoolhouse** was erected in 1896. The simple, one-story wooden-frame building included a central, moderately pitched roof and horizontal lap siding. In 1960 the abandoned building was moved to Rollinsville, the first of four moves over the next several years. At Rollinsville the historic school structure served as the station for the volunteer fire department. A large double door was fitted into one end of the building to accommodate the fire truck. The building was then moved to Gap Road, near the remains of the old Thorn Lake mining camp, where

The Gilpin County School in Central City is now a museum. AUTHOR'S COLLECTION

it again served as a station for that fire department district. After a few years the building was used for storage. Over time and ravaged by harsh weather, the building drastically deteriorated. In 2007 the building was donated to Gilpin County, which promptly added the historic structure to their list of Gilpin County Landmarks on April 3, 2007.[9] The building was moved back to Rollinsville.

Today the historic Thorn Lake Schoolhouse sits on a trailer near Tolland Road in Rollinsville. It is on private property. It is the goal of the Gilpin County Historical Society to eventually restore the last one-room schoolhouse in the county to its former glory.

Rollinsville also hosts the **Tolland School**, appropriately named, as the school was built along Tolland Road. Located in a beautiful meadow along South Boulder Creek, the one-room clapboard schoolhouse was constructed in 1902. Atop the stone foundation, the building included four rectangular windows on each side. The blue metal gabled roof supported an open belfry above the entrance. For several decades the Tolland School served the area, including the settlements of Tolland and

An early-days class photo. CARNEGIE LIBRARY FOR LOCAL HISTORY–BOULDER

Baltimore. Today the schoolhouse, located at Tolland and East Portal Roads, is privately owned. It is listed with the Gilpin County Landmarks, a multiple listing included in the Multiple Property Listings with the Colorado History Center.

Jackson County

In Jackson County, the small community of Coalmont was named for the coal strip mine located in the area. Coalmont was also the end of the line for the Laramie, Hahns Peak & Pacific Railroad. The railroad company originally planned to build to Hahns Peak north of Steamboat Springs, but by 1911 tracks only reached to Coalmont before the company ran out of capital. In 1915 the coal mining community raised funds to build the **Coalmont Schoolhouse** (1018 Jackson CR 26, Coalmont). It was actually the second school in the area and was enlarged when the Hebron School was moved next to the new building. The school served the community until its closure in 1945.

By 1970 the coal deposit was exhausted, and the rails of the Laramie, Hahns Peak & Pacific Railroad were later removed. The Coalmont Schoolhouse was restored in 1997 by the Spicer Club, with funding from the State Historical Fund.

The Coalmont Schoolhouse. KENNETH JESSEN

Jefferson County

During the Pikes Peak gold rush of 1859, a town was laid out near Clear Creek. Located between North and South Table Mountains, it was originally called Golden City. The city became the capital of the federally recognized Colorado Territory in 1862, and the territorial legislature met here until 1867. When Colorado became a state in 1876, the capital moved to Denver. The city shortened its name to Golden and continued to grow. While industry was booming in Golden, the city was also becoming an important center of intellectual development. In 1866 Bishop George M. Randall arrived in the territory and soon began planning for a university that would include two schools.

In 1870 construction commenced on Jarvis Hall, Golden's first institution of higher learning, just south of downtown. While under construction, a severe windstorm tore through the un-boarded window openings of Jarvis Hall, blowing off the roof, collapsing the walls, and delaying completion. Undaunted, Randall soon had hammers and nails swinging again.

On September 3, 1873, the School of Mines opened under the auspices of the Episcopal Church and as an affiliate of Jarvis Hall. Randall lived long enough to see his vision realized, but not long enough to enjoy it; he died three weeks later, on September 28, at the age of sixty-three.

The school administration faced political backlash in 1874 when opinion pieces were published in both the *Rocky Mountain News* and the *Colorado Transcript* opposed to the fact that public funds were being used to support the School of Mines, then owned by the Episcopal Church. The controversy was brought to a close when the **Colorado School of Mines** (1500 Illinois St., Golden) became a territorial institution, the Territorial School of Mines, later that year, and it has been a state institution since 1876, when Colorado attained statehood. However, the school administration faced political backlash when opinion pieces were published in both the *Rocky Mountain News* and the *Colorado Transcript* opposed to the fact that public funds were being used to support the School of Mines, then owned by the Episcopal Church. The controversy was brought to a close in 1874 when the territorial government acquired the school, creating the Territorial School of Mines, Colorado's first public institution of higher education. Due to the state's major industry of gold and silver mining, the first classes offered dealt with mining these particular ores. Later, courses in chemistry, metallurgy, mineralogy, mining engineering, geology, botany, math, and drawing were offered. The first diplomas were awarded in 1882, and the school awarded a diploma to its first female student in 1898.

From 1890 to 1907, enrollment at Mines grew from 65 to 298. To accommodate the needs of a growing campus, **Guggenheim Hall** was added in 1906. Funding for the building came from an $80,000 donation by Simon Guggenheim, a wealthy Denver businessman, politician, and philanthropist whose family made their fortune in mining and smelting. It was the largest monetary gift to a state institution at the time. The building provided students with a new library, more classrooms, and an auditorium. With its stately proportions and skyward golden-domed tower visible from town, it immediately became the central focal point of

One of the first buildings on the campus of the Colorado School of Mines. DENVER PUBLIC LIBRARY

The Guggenheim Building at the Colorado School of Mines.
AUTHOR'S COLLECTION

the campus and continues to be an iconic symbol of the School of Mines. The golden dome is one of the most photographed landmarks on campus.

Around the turn of the twentieth century, a boom in the assaying business prompted construction of a new assay building and lab renovations. Funding came from the school's first monetary gift of $25,000 from Winfield S. Stratton, chairman of the board of trustees and a former student. A mining magnate and Cripple Creek's first millionaire with his Independence Mine, Stratton gave the check to President Regis Chauvenet to use as needed. The state later reimbursed funds for the Assay Building, freeing the gift to go toward construction of Stratton Hall in 1904. In 1950 the Assay Building and adjacent heating plant were joined and the building was renamed Chauvenet Hall.

A portion of Berthoud Hall was designed to house the Colorado School of Mines Geology Museum. Included was an extensive collection of rocks and minerals begun by Professor Arthur Lakes before the split with Jarvis Hall. As early as 1876, the collection won national recognition when Lakes came away from the grand Centennial Exposition in Philadelphia with an award for "Best Geological Exhibit." In 2002 the museum was moved to a new facility at Maple and 13th Streets, where visitors can also view meteorites and a moon rock alongside the most comprehensive collection of Colorado specimens.

Today the school is home to more than two dozen research centers, including the Advanced Control of Energy and Power Systems Center, the Center for Wave Phenomena, and the Colorado Institute for Fuels and High-Altitude Engine Research. The Colorado School of Mines is a public research university focused on science and engineering where students and faculty together address the great challenges related to energy and the environment. The institution is part of Golden's 12th Street Historic District.

Moffat County

Following the Thornburgh Battle and subsequent Meeker Massacre in 1879, military camps were established in northwestern Colorado as the relocation of the Ute to a Utah reservation was underway. One of those camps was in today's Moffat County. Under the command of Lieutenant McCalla the camp was named Camp Lay. The nearby creek was eventually named Lay Creek. In 1881 cattle baron Ora Haley established a post office, and the town of Lay, Colorado, came into being.

The **Lay Schoolhouse** (7 Eddy Ave., Lay) was built in 1910. The one-room building, constructed atop a concrete foundation with windows on all four sides, was built in the modest early twentieth-century American Movements style. Student enrollment that first year was twenty pupils. The school served the students of the community and surrounding area for nearly fifty years. When it was closed due to consolidation in 1959, the community took over the building. The Lay Schoolhouse then served as a community center until the 1980s. When the historic schoolhouse was under consideration for historic preservation status, the *Craig Daily Press* wrote about the history of the town and the significance of the dilapidated schoolhouse. The following paragraph of the September 25, 2009, article is particularly interesting:

Today, the Lay Schoolhouse sits with broken windows and a sagging roof. Barn swallows have taken the place of students and old textbooks molder in a corner of the classroom. Faded 4H pledge banners still hang on the wall and someone's birthday greeting is still scrawled on the worn blackboard. The swing set still stands firm, but seatless, with hand-forged fittings that have worn into the dark smoothness of old iron.

Nearly three years later the Lay Schoolhouse was listed as a historic property on both the state and national registers.

In the northwest corner of Moffat County, Colorado, is the small, isolated community of Brown's Park. In 1910 the **Ladore School** (off County Road 318, eighty-five miles west of Craig, five miles from Gates of Ladore Canyon) was built near the Green River. The log schoolhouse, fifty by thirty feet in size, included an open bell cupola atop the hipped roof. When the building was completed, Frank Meyers, a local rancher, built a small log cabin near the school, which housed many of the students from outlying areas during the school session. The school served the educational needs of students until 1947. Today Ladore School serves as a community center for the residents of Brown's Park.

Rio Blanco County

South of the county line, the historic **Buford School** (40905 CR 17, Meeker) stands in Rio Blanco County. Located in the White River Valley, the schoolhouse was constructed in 1902. Today the building serves as a community center.

The **Coal Creek School** (617 CR 6, Meeker) was built in rural Rio Blanco County in 1892. The one-room schoolhouse was built of local sandstone. A coal shed was built on the property, which also included a privy. A small horse barn was also erected for the students' horses.

In the town of Meeker, the county seat of Rio Blanco County, the **Rio Blanco County High School** (555 Garfield St., Meeker) was constructed in 1924. The two-story building, built of local sandstone, included a gymnasium wing. The school served the community until its closure in 1951.

CoalCreek School (probably school yr. 1896-97) Mrs. Henick, teacher

Schoolchildren at the Coal Creek School. RIO BLANCO HISTORICAL SOCIETY

The Coal Creek School today. RIO BLANCO HISTORICAL SOCIETY

Routt County

Several historic schoolhouses are within the boundaries of Routt County. The small community of Hahns Peak Village, established by Joseph Hahn in 1865, served as the first county seat of Routt County. In 1911 the citizens erected a one-room school known as **Hahns Peak Schoolhouse** (Routt County Road 129 and Main St., Hahns Peak Village, Clark). The typical clapboard building featured an open bell tower. The first schoolmarm, Augusta de Forrest, taught grades one through twelve. Over the years, buildings were added, including a coal shed and a barn for the students' horses. Following the school's closure in 1942, the building was used as a community center.

In 1973 the Hahns Peak Schoolhouse was restored with grants from the Colorado Historical Society. The historic structure was placed on the National Register of Historic Places as well as on the list of Rural School Buildings in Colorado in 1974. Today the Hahns Peak Schoolhouse serves as the Hahns Peak Area Historic Museum.

The **Mesa Schoolhouse** (34191 US Hwy. 40, Steamboat Springs) was built in 1916. The first school built in the new Mesa School District,

Schoolchildren playing in the snow. HAHNS PEAK HISTORICAL SOCIETY

the Mesa School was a large single-story clapboard building. Located in the Yampa Valley area, the school received students from various immigrant families, including some French, German, and Swiss. The school also became the community's social center. The Mesa Schoolhouse closed in 1959 and was then rented as a facility for weddings and social gatherings for the next thirty years. In 1990 the City of Steamboat Springs, in conjunction with Historic Routt County, acquired the schoolhouse with the aid of a grant from the Colorado Historical Society.

In 1914 Charlotte Perry and Portia Mansfield established the **Perry-Mansfield School and Camp** (40755 CR 36, Steamboat Springs), a dance camp in Routt County. Several log cabins were constructed on the property. Still in operation, the Perry-Mansfield School and Camp is the oldest continuously operating modern dance camp in America.

In 1907 the coal mining town of Oak Creek was established in Routt County. Laid out in a grid formation in Oak Creek Canyon, the town became the second-largest in the county following the arrival of the railroad in 1909.

The **Foidel Canyon School** (junction of County Roads 27 and 33, Oak Creek) was erected northwest of town in 1923. The simple clapboard

Eager students ready to learn. RIO BLANCO COUNTY HISTORICAL SOCIETY

structure included a steep-pitched roof that supported an open belfry. In 1928 a two-story, beige brick building was erected to serve as the high school for the area's students. Respected Denver architect Temple Hoyne Buell designed the structure in the Neoclassical Beaux Arts style of the 1920s. Located on private land, both Oak Creek schoolhouses are listed under the Rural School Buildings in Colorado.

Summit County

The small supply town of Dillon, in Summit County, was established in 1879. The town seemed to struggle and was eventually moved near the Blue River. Following the arrival of the Denver & Rio Grande Railroad in 1880, the settlement of Dillon again moved, this time closer to the railroad tracks. In 1883 the Dillon Schoolhouse was erected. Constructed in typical Carpenter's Clapboard style, the building included rectangular windows and a double-door entrance. The A-framed shingle roof supported an open belfry topped with a shingled flared roof. During the 1940s the Denver Water Department began buying land and water rights at various points along the Blue River. Aided by the government's Works Progress Administration (WPA) program, plans were soon in place to build a reservoir. Once again, the town of Dillon moved, this time uphill from the dam site to the old Fred Phillips Ranch.[10]

Among the many buildings moved to the new townsite was the **Dillon Schoolhouse** (405 LaBonte St., Dillon). After the school closed in 1910, the building was used as the community church. Today the historic Dillon Schoolhouse is the home of the Summit Historical Museum. Operated by the Summit County Historical Society, the museum includes a fabulous display of the original McGuffey desks, as well as McGuffey readers used by students. The schoolhouse is included on the National List of Endangered Properties.

Approximately three miles west of Dillon, the town of Frisco was platted in 1879 as a railroad stop for the Denver & Rio Grande Railroad. In 1902 the local saloon, constructed in 1900, was acquired by the town fathers to serve as the school, serving the community until 1958. When the Frisco Historical Society took possession of the one-room clapboard building, it was moved to the Frisco Historic Park. Extensive renovations

An updated school interior. AUTHOR'S COLLECTION

took place, including new gingerbread shingles and an open bell tower. The bell was acquired from a demolished school in Breckenridge. Today the refurbished **Frisco Schoolhouse** (120 Main St., Frisco) serves as the Frisco Historical Society Museum, located in Frisco Park.

The silver mining camp of Montezuma was established in 1865 near the headwaters of the Snake River in Summit County. In 1884 the **Montezuma Schoolhouse** (5375 Webster St., Montezuma) was erected in the center of town. The one-room clapboard structure was built atop a stone foundation. Features of the building included a cupola and a vestibule. Two outhouses were built behind the schoolhouse. Inside, the otherwise plain walls were enhanced with wainscoting. An elevated wooden platform was built, where the teacher taught the students. Verna Sharp was the last teacher when the school closed in 1958. When the Summit County Historical Society restored the historic building, the 1958 Dupont Explosives wall calendar remained intact.

Notes

1. Davis, *Glory Colorado!*, 35.
2. Georgetown Heritage Center archives.
3. Colorado Preservation Inc. Endangered Places Program for the year 2006.
4. *Mountain Music Arts & Culture* magazine, September 5, 2015.
5. Ibid.
6. The George Rowe Museum, housed in the former Silver Plume School, contains one of the finest school room exhibits in the state. The original artifacts, desks, slates, books, and ink quills contribute to an excellent example of a typical nineteenth-century classroom.
7. Granruth, *Central City, Colorado 1859–1999*, 115.
8. Norman and Jones, *Up the Gulch*, 87.
9. Linda Jones, past president of the Gilpin County Historical Society.
10. Summit County Historical Society.

Chapter Nine

Frontier Teacher Mary Ann Rippon

Mary Ann Rippon was not only one of the first three professors at the University of Colorado in Boulder, in 1878 she was the first and only woman.

Born on May 25, 1850, in Lisbon Center, Illinois, Mary was orphaned at an early age. Following the death of her father, Thomas F. Rippon, when she was still a baby, her mother, Jane, was unable to care for her, so Mary was passed from one household to another in the Rippon family. When eighteen-year-old Mary graduated from high school in 1868, she inherited the money from the sale of her father's farm.

Mary had intended to use the money to attend the University of Illinois; however, the school did not admit women. Mary spent the next five years in Europe, where she attended classes at various universities in France, Germany, and Switzerland. In 1873 Mary returned to Illinois. A year later she received an offer to teach in a high school in Detroit, Michigan. Although it was a four-year contract and Mary had never been to Detroit, she accepted the position.

With the opening of the University of Colorado in Boulder in 1877, Joseph Sewall, Mary's former chemistry instructor in Illinois, became the president of the university. Shortly thereafter, Sewall invited Mary to join the CU faculty. Because Mary had one year left on her teaching contract, she declined the offer. Nevertheless, she thought about the opportunity and discussed it among her colleagues. A minister friend of hers who had recently returned from Boulder, warned her of what he considered a deplorable place:

Mary Rippon caused a scandal while teaching at the University of Colorado, but she weathered the storm to become a well-respected teacher. CARNEGIE LIBRARY FOR LOCAL HISTORY–BOULDER

The University of Colorado consisted of a single building located way out on the prairie, and this one building would soon fall down and kill all within it.[1]

When she completed her contractual obligation in Detroit, Mary wired her old friend Joseph Sewall, who again extended the invitation to join the CU faculty. Mary accepted and in January 1878 boarded a train in Detroit for Cheyenne, Wyoming. There she boarded a train and traveled south to Boulder. Mary later recalled her arrival in Boulder:

I was almost alone in the Pullman [car] when the train stopped. Dr. Sewall was there to meet me. The daylight had faded but a new

> *moon cast enough light to show up the wonderful line of the snow clad mountains. The air was that of a perfect January evening, clear, dry and bracing. One of the first questions Dr. Sewall asked me was "How does it look to you?" With eyes turned to the silhouette at the west, and thoughts of the Alps, my one word was "glorious." The genial Doctor relaxed at once as he remarked, "Well, my spirits have risen a hundred percent. My wife had told me you would not stay two days in this lonely place."*[2]

Mary Rippon, the first female professor at the University of Colorado, joined the faculty, which included Dr. Sewall, who taught botany and chemistry as well as serving as president of the institution, and Professor Justin Dow, who taught Greek and Latin. Mary taught French, German, English grammar, and mathematics. Her salary was $1,200 a year. Mary quickly became a role model for the female students on campus.

During her second year as teacher, Mary was observed and evaluated regarding her teaching ability and performance. The CU Board of Examiners noted the following in their report: "Rippon did praiseworthy work in teaching the French and German languages. The tact and zeal she displays in her vocation deserves acknowledgement."[3]

With a recommendation from the Board of Examiners, Mary was promoted to professor of French and German in 1881. Despite the fact that she herself had never earned a college degree, Mary became the first woman in American history to become a full professor at a state university.

Within twelve years, Mary became the chair of the Language Department. Because she was the first female instructor at CU and had accomplished so much, Mary was often the subject of news articles in the *Boulder Daily Camera*.

Despite her popularity with the students and the Boulder community, Mary was the epitome of the spinster teacher and led a somewhat reclusive personal life. It was a time during the Victorian era when there were few professional positions available to women. What's more, according to the custom of the day, women who did manage to secure such a position were not permitted to marry. In 1887 this proved to be a problem for Mary Rippon.

Prior to 1887, Mary had lived as a boarder with several families, as was customary of new teachers in a community. With a full professorship and increased salary, she was able to purchase her own home, a modest Victorian cottage located at 2463 Twelve Street. But 1887 was also the year that Mary began a secret affair with one of her students, William Cephas Housel. Twelve years younger than Mary, Housel was the son of prominent Boulder County judge Peter Housel. Within a year, thirty-seven-year-old Mary was pregnant. She hastily arranged for a sabbatical in Germany. In June, Mary and Housel left Boulder on separate trains and met in St. Louis, Missouri. There, on June 9, 1888, at the Recorder of Deeds office, the couple applied for and received a marriage license. The two were married that afternoon but would keep the marriage secret. From St. Louis the newlyweds traveled to Illinois, where they spent time with Mary's family. In July the couple took separate travel paths. Housel returned to Boulder to finish his final semester, and Mary took a train to New York, where she boarded a ship bound for Germany.

In Germany, Mary occupied her time by writing letters to friends and family. She also managed to maintain the secret of her personal situation by writing letters to Boulder's *County Herald* newspaper. The paper reported in the January 9, 1889, issue that "Miss Rippon is now in Stuttgart, Germany."

On January 17, Mary Rippon Housel gave birth to a girl she named Miriam Edna Housel. Mary sent word to the university that her return trip would be delayed due to illness. The monthly campus newspaper, *University Portfolio*, included a notice in the February 1889 issue regarding the popular teacher's health:

> *On account of ill health, our Professor in French and German, Miss Rippon, is spending a year abroad. May her speedy recovery cause her to return to us at an early day, in safety and happiness.*

Meanwhile, Mary's secret husband, Will Housel, graduated from the university at the end of the spring 1889 semester. Shortly thereafter

Housel sailed for Europe. Arriving in Germany in June, he was reunited with his wife and met his baby daughter for the first time. In Germany, Mary and Will faced a very difficult choice. Mary desperately wanted to return to her position at the University of Colorado but could not do so with a husband and child. Will wanted to pursue his graduate work in Europe. The couple found a compromise whereby both could continue with their individual goals and desires. Baby Miriam was placed in a Catholic orphanage in Germany, and Housel made plans to enroll at a nearby university for his graduate degree. Mary would return to Boulder, Colorado, and her beloved CU.

In June, Mary wrote to the university again with information on her return. The Delta Gamma sorority announced the impending return of their teacher and mentor in their June 1889 newsletter, the *Anchora*. Some of the verbiage and sentiment is ironic given the secret life Mary was then living.

> *With pleasure we learn that Miss Mary Rippon will be with us again next year. Our institution has been long enough without a mother, and orphandom has been sorely felt in many ways. Pretty souvenirs postmarked "Geneva" only prove once more the interest Miss Rippon ever takes in her students. Bright or dull, rich or poor, it matters not. All receive like attention. Do you wonder that we deplore her vacancy in the faculty and long for her return?*

On August 3, Mary left her husband and child in Germany. In Belgium she boarded the SS *Belgenland*, bound for New York. When Mary finally arrived back in Boulder, she received a warm welcome from her many students. The August 14, 1889, issue of the *Boulder County Weekly Herald* reported on Mary's return:

> *Mary Rippon, Professor of German and French, has been connected with the University eleven years. Professor Rippon is returning from her second extended trip to Germany and France and will give to the students the benefit of her mature and cultivated mind.*

In 1901 Mary became dean of women on campus. She formed women's leagues, including the YWCA. One admiring female student wrote:

> *Beautiful Mary Rippon was like a piece of Dresden, but she must have had a stern jaw to be dean of women in those early days.*[4]

Over the next two years, Mary sent money in the form of francs to Will in Germany. The money was used for her husband's school tuition as well as for young Miriam's care. In December, Will returned to Boulder, leaving Miriam in Germany. For the next two years the couple resumed their marital relations, although they never lived together. Mary wrote in her diary, "We had long, sad talks but my job—and secret—were secure."

Following the death of his mother, Will inherited his mother's horses. Will's father, Peter Housel, requested his son's help on the family ranch. Will left Boulder and Mary to join his father. Shortly thereafter, William C. Housel filed for divorce. He eventually remarried and had four children. Will also reclaimed Miriam and raised her within his new family. Mary was allowed to visit when she could, and Miriam came to know her as "Aunt Mary." Mary never remarried.

In July 1909, after thirty-one years at the University of Colorado, Mary Rippon resigned due to ill health. The front page of the *Boulder Daily Camera*, dated July 14, carried the headline "Miss Rippon Resigns After Long Service." The accompanying article read in part: "Her successor has not as yet been chosen. Miss Rippon's unremitting labors have rendered her ill and she is spending the summer in bed at her home on Twelve Street. A more lovable personality and teacher cannot be found in any institution of learning."

The accolades continued. The campus publication *Silver and Gold* dated September 16, 1909, wrote:

> *The long years of continued service brought on ill health which was the cause of her resignation. By her untiring energy as a teacher and her lovable personality, she has brought the German Department to its present high standing and popularity, and all who knew her will be sorry to learn of her departure from the university.*

After relinquishing her teaching position, Mary lived alone in the Victorian cottage she had purchased several decades earlier. Mary continued to send money intended as child support for Miriam to Will Housel. In 1910 Mary paid the tuition for twenty-one-year-old Miriam to attend the University of Michigan.

Within a year Miriam fell in love with her German literature instructor, twenty-four-year-old Rudolf Rieder. When Miriam discovered she was pregnant, the two were secretly married. It was shades of her mother's experience twenty years earlier.

On April 25, 1911, Miriam gave birth to a boy named Walfried Wolf Rieder. Mary sent money to the couple, as well as two life insurance policies she had purchased.[5]

Eventually Miriam returned to school, earning a Bachelor of Arts degree in French in June 1915. This is one accomplishment her "Aunt Mary" never pursued. In 1918 Miriam divorced her husband and retained sole custody of their son, whose name she changed to Wilfred.

In 1920 Miriam and her son arrived in Boulder, where Miriam accepted a teaching position at the University of Colorado. Over the next decade, Mary and Miriam visited but were never close. Mary's secret remained hers alone.

On the morning of September 9, 1935, Mary Ann Rippon died in her Boulder home. She was eighty-five years old. The *Boulder Daily Camera* ran her obituary in that day's issue:

> *Miss Mary Rippon, 85, member of the University of Colorado faculty from the second semester of its opening year to her retirement in the summer of 1909, died this morning at 6:30 at her home, 2463 Twelve Street. Death came peacefully, in keeping with the quiet life she had led since retiring from teaching—a profession that she honored. Miss Rippon never lost interest in the university or her former students. No teacher had more friends. Mrs. Miriam Rieder, assistant professor in Romance languages at the University, was one of Miss Rippon's greatest friends, and Mrs. Rieder's son, Wilfred, was her protege.*

It is clear Mary took her secret to the grave. Mary's funeral was held in her home, with burial in Boulder's Columbia Cemetery.

Not long after her death, a committee was formed at CU to plan a permanent memorial to the frontier teacher. In 1936 the Mary Rippon Theatre was built. The outdoor theater, with twenty rows of sandstone benches, became a popular venue on campus, offering plays, concerts, and other cultural events.

In 1985 Mary Rippon was inducted into the Colorado Women's Hall of Fame. In 1987, an elderly gentleman named Wilfred Rieder donated personal items, including photographs and diaries belonging to Mary Rippon, to the Nolan Library at the University of Colorado. Librarians were stunned when Mr. Rieder revealed that he was Mary Rippon's grandson. Yet the diaries told the story of the secret Mary Rippon kept throughout her lifetime.

In 1998, Sylvia Pettem, Boulder historian and Mary Rippon's biographer, led a movement to have the administration of CU honor Mary Rippon with a college degree, something she never achieved during her lifetime. Finally, on May 12, 2006, Mary Rippon was posthumously granted an honorary degree.

Notes

1. Archives of the University of Colorado, Mary Rippon collection.
2. Ibid.
3. Ibid.
4. Pettem, *Separate Lives, The Story of Mary Rippon*, 84.
5. Ibid., 143.

Chapter Ten

Hey, Diddle, Diddle; the Cat and the Fiddle

Counties South of Interstate 70

Alamosa County

The **Mt. Pleasant School** (junction of County Roads 3S and 103S, eight miles west of Alamosa) in Alamosa County was the only school serving the rural area for nearly eighty years. The current one-room schoolhouse is the third building erected on the site. The one-story structure was built of local sandstone atop a concrete foundation in 1911. The focal point of the building was the corner entrance topped with an open belfry. The schoolhouse served the area until it was closed in 1965. The Mt. Pleasant School is the last remaining one-room schoolhouse in the county.

Chaffee County

The small farming and ranching community of Nathrop was established in 1874 by Charles Nachtrieb, who also built the first flour mill in this area of Chaffee County. In 1881 architect Richard Weeks of nearby Buena Vista built the **Nathrop Schoolhouse** in the center of town at a cost of $2,145. The one-room Carpenter's Clapboard building was erected atop a native stone foundation. Arched windows graced the exterior of the building. Inside, the teacher taught the students from a raised wooden platform. The Nathrop Schoolhouse served the community until 1946. The schoolhouse sat empty for the next ten years. On August 22,

1956, the Gas Creek Extension Homemakers purchased the building, and since then the historic school building has served as the community center.

Just a few miles south of Nathrop, on the west side of US Highway 285, is the historic **Gas Creek School** (junction of County Road 280 and US Highway 285, Nathrop). The land for the schoolyard was donated by a local family by the name of Donley in 1890, with the stipulation that the land would revert to the family if the school closed. The school was built of brick and included a belfry with bell atop the A-frame portion of the roof.[1] When the school opened in 1891, the teacher and her students planted a willow tree in the schoolyard and buried a jar containing the names of the teacher and students near the tree. The Gas Creek School operated until 1942, at which time the land and school property reverted to the Donley family. Today the historic schoolhouse is well preserved, as is the surrounding schoolyard, complete with the original swing set and outhouse.

The **Poncha Springs Schoolhouse** (330 Burnett St., Poncha Springs) was built in the small community of Poncha Springs. Completed in 1883, the two-story redbrick building was designed in the Italianate style. A cross-gabled roof supported an open bell tower with a mansard roof. Inside, there were two classrooms on the first floor and offices and an auditorium on the second floor. After seventy years of service, the Poncha Springs Schoolhouse closed in 1957. In 1962 the town of Poncha Springs acquired the schoolhouse, which has served the community as a museum ever since.

In the southwest portion of Chaffee County, the **Maysville School** (south of US Highway 50, Maysville) was constructed in 1912. The one-room clapboard schoolhouse included a steep pitched roof that supported an open belfry in the center. Inside, the single classroom was located at one end of the building; the teacher's living quarters occupied the other end. Following the school's closure in 1939, the building served as a community center for several years. In 1977 the Salida Museum Association purchased the schoolhouse. The building is listed with the Rural School Buildings in Colorado as well as on the National Register.

Just west of the town of Salida, the **Valley View School** (County Road 140, two miles west of Salida) was built in 1903. The single-story wood-framed building served as the educational facility as well as the community center. In 1936 the Works Progress Administration (WPA) constructed a concrete block addition to the schoolhouse that included separate privies for boys and girls.

In 1922 architects Francis W. Cooper and Leo A. Desjardins designed Salida's new school. Located at the corner of Ninth and D Streets, the two-story blond-brick building was erected atop a concrete foundation. Upon completion in 1923, the **Kesner Memorial Building** (East 9th Street and C Street, Salida) went on to serve generations of Salida students for the next several decades.

Custer County

The town of Westcliffe, in Custer County, was created by William A. Bell, vice president of General William Jackson Palmer's Denver & Rio Grande Railroad, and became the county seat of Custer County in 1881. Ten years later, in 1891, the **Westcliffe School** (304 4th St., Westcliffe) was built at the northwest corner of Powell Avenue and 4th Street. The one-room schoolhouse was constructed of local lava stone. Fish-scale shingles enhanced the rooftop, which supported the bell tower. Following the closure of the school in 1953, the building was eventually restored and became the town's community center.

In 1889 a one-room clapboard schoolhouse was constructed in the rural area of the county. Located at the junction of two roads that would later be named Schoolfield Lane and Willow Lane, the **Willows School** (Willow Lane, between Muddy and Schoolfield Lanes, Westcliffe) served the area until its closure in 1948. At that time, the building became a center for community events.

Tucked within a grove of ponderosa pine on the west side of the Wet Mountain Valley area in Custer County is the charming one-room log cabin schoolhouse aptly named the Pine Grove School.

The area was originally settled by German immigrants and was known as the Colfax Colony in Custer County. When a school district was established in 1890, Willis Ackelbein donated a plot of his original homestead claim for the building of the school. The log schoolhouse was built by locals and served their children's learning needs through the eighth grade.

At the beginning of each school term, one of the older boys was selected to be responsible for heating the school building. The boy would arrive early and stoke the fire, adding more wood to the stove as needed. For this chore, the boy was paid $1 a week. Another student would be assigned the duty of carrying the water bucket to the nearby Canda family residence to be filled with fresh water. A single dipper was shared among all the children. When this resulted in the rapid spread of colds or the flu among the children, parents insisted on having their child bring their own water to school.

In 1902 the Canda family purchased the Ackelbein homestead and the school was renamed the **Canda School** (County Road 130/Horn Road, a half mile west of County Road 129). The school closed in the late 1940s with the consolidation of rural schools in Custer County. Today the one-room log schoolhouse sits empty at the base of the Sangre de Cristo Mountains, whose peaks tower over fourteen thousand feet. It is located on private land but can easily be photographed from the public road without trespassing. It is listed under the Rural School Buildings in Colorado.

Fremont County

The town of Cañon City, the county seat of Fremont County, claims four historic schools. The **Garden Park School** (5800 Garden Park Rd., Cañon City) was built just outside town in 1893. The Garden Park area was designated as School District #5 at that time. The single-story building was constructed of adobe bricks formed from the clay at nearby Oil Creek. Local residents assisted in the making of the bricks. The adobe bricks were designed to make the building resistant to fire. The school officially opened in 1895 with forty-eight students.

The first teacher was Eva Serena Sadoris. Sadoris boarded with various families, as was the custom for single female teachers. Married women were not allowed to teach until 1934. The school year lasted from Labor Day to mid-May, with time off during the harvest so students

The schoolhouse in Garden Park. GOLD BELT TOUR SCENIC AND HISTORIC BYWAY

could help their families with the crops. The school held a community picnic in May to mark the end of the year. An article from the *Cañon City Daily Record* dated February 5, 1883, stated that the school, under the tutelage of Mr. H. Newberry, had closed after a four-month term. "The district is small and hence for want of funds, can never have more than from four to six months of schooling during a year."

As the only public building for miles around, the school served as an important community center, hosting Sunday school meetings, dances, theatrical productions, and other local events. The *Fremont County Sun* published an article about the Garden Park School. Dated April 25, 1979, the piece included remembrances from former students such as Eric Freek, who said, "The building was used for 'literaries,' dances and Sunday school."

Additional facilities built over the years included outhouses, a stable, a baseball diamond, and playground equipment. The *Cañon City Daily Record* noted in their April 28, 1926, issue: "The Garden Park ball team played the Cañon City High School team on the Garden Park diamond. The score was 10 to 6 in favor of the Garden Park team."

Over time the adobe brick proved to be susceptible to deterioration. To protect the adobe from the elements, local rancher Luther Langford covered the brick walls with stucco in 1916–1917. Other alterations during the school's tenure included the addition of concrete steps at the front entry and relocation of the building's chimney from the west wall to the east wall when the original heating stove was replaced. The building was not wired for electricity until 1951.

The one-room schoolhouse served the community until consolidation in 1961. Then children were bused ten miles to schools in Cañon City. For decades the Garden Park School stood as a vacant landmark along a bend in Garden Park Road, ten miles north of Cañon City in what is now the **Gold Belt Scenic and Historic Byway**. As of this writing, the building is being renovated for community purposes.

On the west side of Cañon City is the storied **Mount Saint Scholastica** building (615 Pike Ave., Cañon City). Originally built as a military school in 1881, the three-story Victorian building located at Pike and Seventh Streets served the community for 111 years.

The Grand Army of the Republic began building their school, known as the Collegiate and Military Institute, in 1880. By summer 1882 the school was nearing completion. The *Fremont County Record* reported the progress in the August 5, 1882, issue:

> *Our new military college building will be ready for the fall term which will begin on September 4th. There will be a good enrollment and many new features introduced that was impossible to attempt in the former contracted quarter. Capt. Henry Curtis, of West Point, will fill the position of adjutant, professor of mathematics and instructor in drill tactics.*

Just before the school was set to open, reporters from the *Fremont County Record* were invited to tour the new facilities in an effort to gain the utmost favorable attention from the community as well as to draw students. The following report appeared in the August 26, 1882, issue:

> *Perhaps few of our citizens are aware of the completeness, convenience and finish of the new military college building. It is a just source of pride and congratulation that the energy and benevolence of some of Cañon's best citizens have worked such results a substantial monument to their faith in the good that educational privileges ensure to the town in which they live and have built their homes. In the basement you enter a hall from which opens on the one side a large room filled up as an armory with a turning or gymnastic bar in the center; it is large enough to drill and exercise in.*
>
> *From this hall you also enter a bath room with hot and cold water faucets, a servants room and an ample dining room; a kitchen with range, reservoir, sink and pantry occupy the balance of the basements, the ceilings high and all the rooms pleasant. The first floor is furnished for the President and his family on one side, the main hall and two school rooms on the other, comprising a study for the young ladies and a primary or preparatory room. Broad stairs, broken by a landing half way up, lead to the second floor, here a hall-way leads on one side to a general school room, occupying the entire width of the building, the center room is in the tower and is the President's office and study; the other side is divided into three apartments to be used as music, art and library rooms. Still following the winding stairway we reach the upper rooms which consist of ten dormitories and an Adjutants room; stationary basins in the hall are supplied with hydrant water. The water pipes are being laid on Seventh Street to connect with the pipes of the college. The grounds graded, leveled and sanded, and it is most sincerely to be hoped that those having these improvements in charge will see that the house is secured against any unexpected or possible rush of water from any and every direction. Men of the commonest experience with adobe soil in Colorado ought not lose sight of this one moment, nor allow a good building to be twenty-four hours without*

sure and sufficient banking about it. From what we hear and can learn we feel sure that the venture of incorporating, supporting and building the Military College in Cañon City is a success.

E. H. Sawyer, a Civil War veteran, was the first school commandant of the Colorado Collegiate and Military Institute, and he along with five teachers oversaw the first class, which consisted of sixty-six students. Students, both boys and girls, were accepted as young as six years of age and required to wear uniforms. Classes included mathematics and commercial science, mining engineering and assaying, art, and general preparatory classes, as well as military tactics.

One of those first students was sixteen-year-old Sarah Felch. Sarah's parents, Marshall and Amanda Felch, were both Civil War veterans who served in the Union Hospital Corps. Marshall had been a hospital steward and Amanda had been a nurse with the resilience and grit to serve her country.

Following the war, the couple moved to Colorado and homesteaded in Garden Park, where they raised their family. Sarah and her three younger brothers, Ned, Webster, and Willie, lived with their parents on a ranch. This location was also known as Paradise Park for its splendor, grandeur, and beauty. The family ranch was about twelve miles from the Colorado Collegiate and Military Institute. Because the Felches could barely afford the school tuition, Sarah was a day student rather than a boarder. This meant that transportation to the school was either by horseback or wagon.

A discovery of dinosaur bones by Marshall and others in 1877 began the notorious "Bones War." Eventually, an eastern museum was awarded the extraordinary find. Sarah and her father had an invested part in cleaning, identifying, and shipping the bones back east.

Unfortunately, financial issues arose shortly after the military institute opened. The Grand Army of the Republic donated $100,000, yet despite the donation, the school did not become financially stable. Financial reports cited that high tuition costs—$600 for the forty-two-week school term—eventually led to the school's closing in 1886. The property reverted to the holding company, Central Colorado Improvement Company, in late 1886.

The Benedictine Sisters of Chicago, a Roman Catholic religious organization whose mission was the establishment of mission schools, bought the property in 1889. In keeping with their religious order, the school became part of the St. Scholastica Academy, named for Scholastica, the twin sister of Saint Benedict, for whom the order was formed. However, after arriving in Cañon City, the Sisters were met with hostility and fear from the community. Storekeepers refused to sell groceries to the nuns. But then, as luck (or divine intervention) would have it, a stray cow wandered onto their property. The nuns were able to milk the cow, providing themselves with some nourishment. Soon local parishioners introduced the nuns to the store owners and guaranteed payment for their purchases. While the nuns were now able to purchase supplies, according to Royal Gorge Regional Museum and History Center records, verbal insults and rocks were thrown at them whenever they walked through town. The *Cañon City Daily Record of* April 12, 1890, reported on the opening of the new school:

> *This Easter review of the religious influence of Cañon City would not be complete without a mention of the Mount St. Scholastica's Academy. This is a religious educational institution of more than local note, and its buildings are some of the most prominent in the city. Mt. St. Scholastica's re-opened in the present building, a structure 72-by-62 feet, possessing all the modern improvements and conveniences. To the north, some feet from the school, is a memorial chapel, the gift of Eugene O'Reilly, of Chicago. This is the most beautiful little chapel in the state. The front porch, recently added to [the] main building, is a magnificent donation of P. J. McCormack, of Guffey. A neat little cottage for the Reverend Chaplain has just been completed in the southern part of the academy grounds. The grounds consist of lawns, promenades, croquet and tennis courts.*

In the fall of 1890, the doors opened at Mount St. Scholastica Academy, welcoming some forty students who made up its first class. However, the success of the school did not last long; in 1892 disaster struck and the school was forced to close. The constant reverberations from construction blasting by the state penitentiary to make way for a new irrigation ditch through the hogbacks severely damaged the building, shattering windows and cracking the walls and making it uninhabitable. Students returned home to their parents and the three nuns lived in makeshift tents on the property until they were able to obtain a small settlement from the state, allowing the needed repairs to be made. A new building was built on the original foundation, and the school reopened five years later, in 1897.

A notable person who visited Colorado between 1902 and 1912, and who stayed in the East Building during her visits to Cañon City, was Sister Frances Xavier Cabrini. While visiting, she slept in the small room with a balcony on the second floor, south side. Later known as Mother Cabrini, in 1946 she was canonized as the first naturalized American saint.

More construction followed, and the school building and residence building were completed in 1900. The West Building housed the study hall, classrooms, dormitories, and recreation areas. Disaster struck again in 1917. The January 11 issue of the *Cañon City Record* reported the story under the headline:

> *FIRE DAMAGES EAST BUILDING OF ACADEMY THIS MORNING*
>
> *The fire originated in the roof at the base of one of the dormer windows on the south side of the structure and was not discovered until after it had made considerable headway, which necessitated an immediate call on the fire department for help to prevent a general conflagration of the academy plant. An alarm was sent in to the Fire Department and prompt response was made to the summons. Attachment of the hose to a conveniently located fire plug was hurriedly made and [in] a few minutes a stream of water was being played on the flames to good advantage. At the time the alarm was given, no one connected with the academy was aware the fire was so close. The first intimation they had was when the firemen pounded on the main door of the east building and demanded admittance to the attic floor.*

Sister M. Agatha, the doorkeeper, admitted the men and then sounded the school alarm. The students were in classes but immediately arose and in an orderly manner marched out of the building. Many who were at the fire remarked at the perfect calmness of the sisters and the girls. They took it as if such a fire was an every day occurrence. The Sisters in the kitchen kept on with their work, with prayers on their lips, declaring the Sisters and girls would have to eat, fire or no fire.

In the late 1930s the elementary grades moved to St. Michael's School and the academy transitioned to a girls-only high school, shortening its name to St. Scholastica Academy. It maintained its mission as a college preparatory school, but St. Scholastica adapted and modified its teaching methods through the years.

In the mid-1990s women's achievements were spotlighted at St. Scholastica Academy with an annual Women's Week dedicated to female leaders, visionaries, and artists, featuring some of the foremost women leaders in the country at the time. In 1996 the leading guest was NASA astronaut Major Nancy Jane Currie. In 1998 the guest speaker list included Linda Tafoy, executive director of the Coors Foundation; poet Naomi Ayala; Holocaust survivor and author Eleanor Ayer; plus several other prominent women.

In February 2001 Sister Jane Smith, prioress of the Benedictine Sisters of Chicago, made the shocking announcement that the graduating class of 2001 would be St. Scholastica's last. The closure was not due to the failure of the mission, as nearly 90 percent of graduates went on to attend college, or financial concerns, as the school had no debt. Rather, the Sisters themselves were diminishing in numbers. This was cited as the primary reason for the closure, as well as a drop in enrollment.

Few buildings of the original school property remain today. However, the main redbrick building with its Queen Anne porch still stands. Known as "Big Red," it is a ghostly reminder of school days gone by.

In 1914 the **South Cañon High School** (1020 Park Ave., Cañon City) was built. The three-story brick building included rectangular windows with sandstone trim. The new school represented the southern faction of students and created a rivalry with North Cañon High School. In 1920 the two schools consolidated, and the former South Cañon High School became the only junior high school in Cañon City for the next forty years.

Following consolidation of the North and South high schools in 1920, the **Madison School** (202 East Douglas Ave., Cañon City) was one of two additional schools built during that era. The one-story brick building is the second-oldest school building in Cañon City.

At the corner of East Main Street and Steinmeier Avenue is the lonely school building known as the **Four Mile School** (East Main Street and Steinmeier Avenue, Cañon City). Built in 1894, it was originally called Fruitmere School. The one-story brick schoolhouse served the students of the community from first through eighth grades. The schoolhouse had two rooms. First through third grades were in one room; fourth through sixth grades were in the other. When the state began the school consolidation process in the 1950s, the seventh and eighth grade students were transported by bus to Roosevelt Junior High. It was during this period that the school changed names from Fruitmere to Four Mile School. Over time, as student enrollment shrank, the school only served kindergarten and first grade. During the 1980s and 1990s the school was used by Head Start, a preschool program, and eventually closed. The school is no longer in use, but the community center is still used for events.

Garfield County

In Garfield County, the community of Carbondale came together to construct a school for their children. The **Missouri Heights School** (County Road 102, Carbondale) was built in 1917. The single-story clapboard building with its steep-pitched roof included five windows on two sides. A separate building served as a teacherage. A coal shed and two outhouses were also constructed. In 1963 the Missouri Heights Community League acquired the property, which is listed on the State and National Registers.

Also in Garfield County, the **Battlement Mesa School** (7201 300 Rd., Battlement Mesa) was established in 1897. The two-room schoolhouse was built of local sandstone from nearby Stone Quarry Creek. The schoolhouse also served as the community center. An addition to the building was constructed in 1907 with the same locally quarried sandstone. The school closed in 1957.

Gunnison County

Gunnison County lays claim to three historic schoolhouses. In 1893 the **Rock Schoolhouse** (507 Maroon Ave., Crested Butte) was built in the mining town of Crested Butte. Located at the southeast corner of Fifth Street and Maroon Avenue, the building was constructed of native stone and featured a front bay that separated the two entrances: one for boys and one for girls. The shingled mansard roof was topped with an open cupola and a weathervane. Today the building serves as the Old Rock Community Library.

The **Marble High School** (412 Main St., Marble) was erected in the small mining town of Marble in 1910. Built atop a marble foundation, the building included square marble posts that supported the porch entry. The gabled roof included an open bell cupola. The two-story clapboard building featured large windows symmetrically arranged. The paint scheme for the building was white and green, the company colors of the Colorado Yule Marble Company.

Today the historic Marble High School serves as the local museum. The town of Marble is listed on the Colorado State Multiple Listing Register as well as the National Register District.

South of US Highway 50, near Curecanti National Recreation Area and Black Canyon of the Gunnison National Park is the **Rimrock School** (County Road 24, Sapinero). Built in 1920, the rural one-room schoolhouse was typical of the era. Behind the schoolhouse, two outhouses were erected. When the school closed in 1946, the building served as a community center. The Rimrock School is listed with the Rural School Buildings in Colorado as well as on the State and the National Registers.

Hinsdale County

In Hinsdale County, the **Debs School** (673 McManus Rd., Pagosa Springs) is the county's only surviving one-room schoolhouse. Built in 1926 in the southeast region of the county, the school was constructed of concrete and rock. Following the school's closure in 1951, the building served as a community center. The Debs School is listed with the Ornamental Concrete Block Buildings of Colorado, the Rural School Buildings in Colorado, and on the National Register.

South of Hinsdale County is the **Chromo School** (US Highway 84, Chromo). The concrete and adobe one-room schoolhouse was built in 1922 and operated as a school until 1954. Characteristics, reminiscent of local Hispanic influence, included a steep pitched roof with an open belfry at the center. A teacherage and outhouse were built behind the school. Today the Chromo School serves as a community center.

Jefferson County

In 1875 the **Morrison Schoolhouse** (226 Spring St., Morrison) was built by town founder George Morrison. The two-story Romanesque-style building was constructed of limestone by the Morrison Stone, Lime & Town Company. Two classrooms, one on each floor, served to educate the local children until 1959. The historic structure was later renovated into a private residence, and a large addition was built in 2006. The school is listed with the Rural School Buildings in Colorado as well as on the National Register.

The small mountain community of Pleasant Park, in Jefferson County, erected a single-story clapboard school in 1894. The **Pleasant Park School** (22551 Pleasant Park Rd., Conifer) served the community for fifty-five years. In 1907 the building served the community as Pleasant Park Grange #156 of the regional farmers associations.

La Plata County

In Durango, the county seat of La Plata, the **Durango High School** (201 East 12th St., Durango) was built in 1917. The Classical Revival style is evident in the building, designed by Colorado Springs architects Thomas MacLaren and Charles Thomas. The three-story blond-brick structure included tall windows enhanced with terra-cotta framing. The stone stairway to the arched entrance included natural stone banisters. The building was the only high school until it was closed in 1976.

The **Smiley Junior High School** (1309 East Third Ave., Durango) was constructed in 1937. MacLaren and Thomas also designed and built this educational facility. Blond brick was used in the three-story structure with elements of the Mission Revival style, such as an arched entrance and decorative parapets. The Smiley Junior High School was the largest building in Durango, constructed with federal funds under the WPA program. After nearly thirty years, the school was closed in 1961.

Mesa County

In Mesa County, the **Fruita Elementary School** (325 East Aspen St., Fruita) was constructed in 1912. The two-story brick building was erected atop the raised basement of the original 1887 structure. Two wings were added in 1936 as part of a project funded by the WPA. The addition served as a junior high annex.

A few miles south of Fruita, the agricultural community of Glade Park constructed their schoolhouse in 1919. The one-room structure was built of logs and included an abundance of windows for lighting. With its proximity to the Utah border, the **Coates Creek Schoolhouse** (D S Road, 16 miles west of Glade Park) attracted several children from Utah. The historic schoolhouse is the only remaining log school building in Mesa County.

Park County

In 1897 the Slaughts Schoolhouse was built a half mile from the small community of Shawnee. Located on Park County Road 64, the small one-room clapboard building with rectangular windows and a front gabled roof hosted children from grades one through eight. As the town population grew, by 1899 the school became known as the Shawnee School. The school closed during World War II. Reopening in 1946, the school served the community for two years before permanently closing in 1948. The schoolhouse was moved into the town, where it was used by the community as a Sunday school. In 1983 the Park County Historical

Society moved the historic **Shawnee School** (McGraw Memorial Park, Bailey) to its present location in McGraw Park, in the town of Bailey.

At the foot of Kenosha Pass, the small town of Jefferson was established as a railroad town for the Denver, South Park & Pacific Railroad Company in 1879. Willard Head, credited with forming the town, built the first hotel, a general store, and a livery stable. Head also spearheaded the building of the first school, **Jefferson Schoolhouse** (100 Main St., Jefferson). The one-room clapboard building was replaced in 1901 with a new schoolhouse. Constructed in the typical Carpenter's Clapboard style of architecture, the building included large rectangular windows and a semigabled roof. Atop the roof a tall belfry was erected over the school entrance. The extended cloakroom entrance protruded from the front of the building. In 1936 an additional building, used as a gymnasium, was erected next to the schoolhouse. After the school closed, the gymnasium building was used for community recreational activities as well as a community center. In the 1990s a kitchen and indoor bathrooms were added.[2]

Students take a break from learning. PARK COUNTY HISTORICAL SOCIETY

Today the Jefferson Schoolhouse is used for Sunday church services, weddings, and funerals.

In the summer of 1879, railroad workers for the Denver, South Park & Pacific Railroad Company erected a campsite at the present site of Como in Park County. On July 2, 1879, the South Park Coal Company filed a town plat application with the Park County Clerk and Recorders Office. By the end of that summer, the railroad company "had completed two short branch lines east and west of the main line to reach the coal mines near Como."[3] By 1882 the DSP&P had completed a branch line to Breckenridge over Boreas Pass and eventually to Leadville. With Como being the division point for the railroad, the population of the town grew to several thousand. With these dramatic accomplishments, Como experienced a remarkable period of prosperity.

It was during this time that the citizens of Como built the **Como School** (165 Spruce St., Como). The one-story Carpenter's Clapboard building included rectangular framed windows as well as a rectangular framed entrance. The gabled roof included a belfry above the entrance. Three teachers were employed to educate the children, divided into

Boys will be boys at the Como School. PARK COUNTY HISTORICAL SOCIETY

elementary, intermediate, and high school classes. Years later, Anna Williamson Stockling recalled her early school years at Como:

> *In 1895 my parents moved from Denver, where I was born, to the mining community of King. My father screened coal from the slag and delivered to customers in Como. Since we children were nearing school age, my parents felt we must move to Como.*[4]

The Como School served the community until 1948. Today the historic schoolhouse, located on Spruce Street, is owned and operated by the Como Civic Association, serving as a town hall for the community.

West of Como and approximately seven miles north of Fairplay, the town of Alma was established on March 7, 1873. Because of the location, at the junction of the South Platte River and Buckskin Creek, Alma served as the supply town for mines of Park County and later became

The Como School today. HEATH GAY

the smelting center of South Park. In 1887 a two-story wooden frame schoolhouse, complete with an enclosed belfry, was built to serve the educational needs of the children of the many families residing in the area. On May 15, 1928, the schoolhouse burned to the ground. The new **Alma School** (59 East Buckskin St., Alma), built in the Mission Revival style, was constructed and opened in time for the fall school term.[5] In 1936, with funds provided by the Works Progress Administration, additional buildings were added, designed and built by Frank Frewen.

Today the Alma School building serves as the Alma Town Hall.

In 1880 the **Fairplay School** (639 Hathaway St., Fairplay) was built in Fairplay. Constructed of native red sandstone, the two-story schoolhouse was built in the Italianate style. Features of this popular Victorian architectural style included a gabled roof with prominent eaves enhanced with roof brackets. Over the years, additions and improvements changed the original integrity of the school's style. The Fairplay School was renamed the Edith Teter Elementary School, for a well-respected longtime teacher. The school is listed on the Colorado Register of Historic Places and among the Park County Historic Landmarks. The historic school continues to serve as an educational institution for the children of Fairplay.

Nine miles east of Fairplay, the **Garo School** was constructed in 1879. The single-story clapboard structure with rectangular windows included a gabled roof over the extended entrance. The building was originally painted red with white trim. By 1900 the schoolhouse had been repainted white. In 1960 the historic building was moved to the South Park City Museum at Fairplay (100 4th St., Fairplay).

Approximately twenty miles southeast of Fairplay, the **Hartsel School** (80 Valley Dr., Hartsel) was built to serve the educational needs of the area's children. A land survey conducted in 1946 revealed that the schoolhouse was situated on private land, so the historic building was moved a single block to the town boundaries of Hartsel. After the statewide school consolidation, the school was closed and students were bused to the schools in Fairplay. Today the Hartsel School building serves the community as the Hartsel Community Center.

The Garo School. PARK COUNTY HISTORICAL SOCIETY

The Hartsel School in Park County. PARK COUNTY HISTORICAL SOCIETY

The small mining community of Puma City was laid out in June 1896. Located approximately twelve miles east of Fairplay and thirteen miles northwest of Lake George, near Tarryall Creek, the town was later renamed for the creek. The first Tarryall schoolhouse was a simple one-room log cabin. Within a year the population had swelled to more than one thousand. In 1898 a new schoolhouse was built a mile north of the original log cabin facility.

In 1921 residents of the community pooled their talents to erect a new **Tarryall School** (31000 Park CR 77, Tarryall).[6] The local sawmill provided the lumber for the one-room clapboard structure. Features included double rectangular windows and single windows on either side of the doorway. The gabled roof supported an open belfry.

Inside, a small kitchen was constructed as well as a space utilized as a cloakroom. Two blackboards, used in the original log cabin schoolhouse, were placed in the new school building. The Tarryall School served as the education center for the community until 1949.

Today, although Tarryall is a ghost town, the building is used as the community center for the surrounding region.

The Tarryall School. PARK COUNTY HISTORICAL SOCIETY

The Tarryall School as it appears today. HEATH GAY

Saguache County

The town of Saguache hosts two historic schools. The Saguache School, constructed in 1874, is perhaps the oldest structure in the community. Surprisingly, in 1908 the City of Saguache built a new jail, which adjoined the school. Nevertheless, the adobe building served the educational needs of the community's children until 1959. Today the **Saguache School & Jail Building** (US Highway 285 and San Juan Avenue, Saguache) serves as the Saguache County Museum.

In 1915 the architectural firm of Manning & Frewen designed and built the **Saguache Elementary School** (605 Christy Ave., Saguache). The brick building is a fine example of Mediterranean Revival style, with round, arched windows and an arched entrance. Another unique feature was the H-shape design of the building.

Located in the foothills of the Sangre de Cristo Mountains, the mining town of Crestone was established in 1880. That same year, the **Crestone School** (Cottonwood Street and Carbonate Avenue, Crestone) was built at the corner of Carbonate Avenue and Cottonwood Street. The single-story, two-room clapboard building was sheathed in board-and-batten siding. The entrance was enhanced by a gabled vestibule. The windows were graced with pedimented lintels. In 1912 an open belfry was erected atop the schoolhouse. The bell, acquired from the C. B. Bell Company of Hillsboro, Ohio, was proudly placed in the belfry.

Changes were made over the years, including the addition of a kitchen. The exterior received a change as well when the board-and-batten siding was replaced with traditional clapboard siding. The entrance to the faculty was enlarged to accommodate caskets for funerals.

After the school closed in 1949, the building became the town's community center. In 1976 the belfry was found to be extremely deteriorated. The bell was removed from the belfry and placed on a rock pedestal next to the school.

Teller County

In Teller County, the ranching community of Florissant was established in 1872 by Judge James Costello. A simple one-room log building served as Florissant's first schoolhouse. In 1885, as railroad tracks for the Colorado Midland Railroad were being laid toward Florissant, several railroad workers brought their families to Florissant.

Because the log schoolhouse could not accommodate the new students, the community began a building fund in 1886. The Costello family sold an acre of their land to School District 13 for $1.[7] The architectural firm of Coldwell & Spoon received the contract for the construction of the new school. The large wood-frame schoolhouse was built with an L-shaped floor plan, its enclosed entry capped with a closed four-sided bell tower with a pyramidal roof. On either side of the entrance, rectangular windows allowed sunlight into the building. Two outhouses were also built. Located behind the schoolhouse, the privies were enhanced by Victorian latticework. The **Florissant School** (2009 CR 31, Florissant) was completed in the fall of 1887, at a cost of just under $1,000.

The original log schoolhouse was sold at auction for $17. It is believed the historic structure was moved near the Florissant Cemetery, although

The Florissant School. HEATH GAY

there is no trace of the building today.[8] Two years later, in 1889, a teacher's residence was built next to the Florissant School building. When the school closed in 1960, the local Grange purchased the building.

Today the Florissant School building retains much of its historic grandeur, including the original interior wainscoting, teacher's desk, student desks, large blackboard, and a piano. It is listed on the National Register of Historic Places, as well as in the Multiple Property Submission with the List of Rural School Buildings in Colorado.

South of Florissant is the historic mountain mining town of Cripple Creek. **Cripple Creek High School** (350 East Carr Ave., Cripple Creek) was one of an astonishing seventeen school sites in the Mining District. Today it is one of only two original schools still standing. The other is Victor High School, located six miles away in the mountain community of Victor.

Cripple Creek High School was built of brick following the devastating fire of April 1896, when nearly two-thirds of the town burned

The interior of the Florissant School as it is today. AUTHOR'S COLLECTION

to the ground. The school was built in two phases. The southern half, or back end, of the school, roughly ninety feet, was built in 1896. Built in the Romanesque architectural style, the structure had a flat roof, stone lintels, and rounded window arches. The lengthy basement foundation followed the sloping hillside and included an enclosed stone staircase to the upper floor and the main entrance. The two-story schoolhouse opened its doors to students in 1897.

In 1901 construction of the northern portion of the building began. The two-story exterior brick walls followed the Romanesque architectural style but, when completed in 1905, included a pitched roof and a square tower. The interior of this portion sported the gym and a large auditorium. An outdoor pool was added in the late 1940s.

Perhaps the school's most famous student was Ralph Carr, 1905. Carr went on to earn a law degree and become state attorney general. In 1938 he was elected governor of Colorado. He was reelected, serving during World War II.

Boys at play in the Cripple Creek schoolyard. DENVER PUBLIC LIBRARY

One of the features of Cripple Creek High School was the outdoor swimming pool. VICTOR LOWELL THOMAS MUSEUM, LEDFORD COLLECTION

The high school served the educational needs of students until 1926, when it became the only school in Cripple Creek, teaching all grades as student enrollment dropped. Peak enrollment was 350 students. Enrollment averaged one hundred students by 1966, and the school closed in 1977.

The school was converted to a small hotel in 1983; twenty years later, new owners completely renovated the building as a boutique hotel and restored its rich history. Today it is known as Carr Manor, for its famed student. The hotel offers thirteen rooms, two suites, and a Grand Ballroom in the old gym.

The Cripple Creek High School building is part of the Cripple Creek Historic District, which received National Historic Landmark status in 1961.

Six miles southwest of Cripple Creek on Colorado Highway 67 is the mountain mining town of Victor. As part of the historic Cripple Creek Mining District, Victor lays claim to the only other historic school building in the district. With the riches of gold produced by the many mines on Battle Mountain above town, the major buildings were rapidly being built of brick. The cornerstone for the new **Victor High School** (100 Dewey St., Victor) was laid on August 28, 1899, exactly one week after a devastating fire consumed nearly all of the town's wood-framed buildings. D. W. McIntosh, contractor for the new school, built the two-story building of red brick on a hill overlooking the east end of town. McIntosh designed the new school to be one of the largest buildings in the rebuilt town, as well as to stand as a monument to education in the mining community. Apparently the students of Victor High felt the same about their school; the following tribute was published in Victor High School's publication, *The Sylvanite*, in the April–May 1909 issue:

The halls of the Victor High School are
more precious to us than jewels or gold,
Is our dear old Victor High.
Our love for her in our hearts we'll hold
And ever her colors fly.
For these colors we'll always fight,

And our efforts will ever be,
To keep them waving high and bright
So that all who come may see.
We are proud of our dear old school,
The grandest in the land;
And we'll obey her every rule
With willing heart and hand.
We'll keep her always in the lead,
The finest, truest and best.
Our dear old Victor High School,
Pride of all the West.
Now, let each one do his part
And loud the chorus swell.
With the sounds so dear to every heart,
The Victor High School yell.

Sports were also an important part of the curriculum at the Victor High School. An excerpt from *The Sylvanite* states:

> *There is not one reason why V.H.S. can not have a winning team.*
>
> *We have the best coach in the district to coach us. Mr. Haspe understands the game thoroughly and is willing to make a winning team out of us if the ways will only come out.*
>
> *One or two boys in the school have got the foolish notion that they know everything about the game and don't need any coaching. Well, let those individuals remember one thing that if that is the spirit they intend to show they are not wanted.*
>
> *This thing has gone so far that one of two things has got to be done. Either we must take hold of this thing and make a winning team or let athletics out altogether and let Victor High be "has-beens."*
>
> *So let every boy in the school who can even lift a ball be out to practice from now on.*

Perhaps the most famous student was Lowell Thomas. A world-famous broadcaster, journalist, and world traveler, Thomas graduated from Victor High School in 1909. His father was the only doctor in

64 THE MINER

The Victor High School basketball team, 1915. MARK PERDEW

Senior Boys' Basket Ball Team.

Roy Grator, captain, is a four year man of great value. He played as a regular on the High School team for two years and would easily have made a forward this year had there been a team.

Clair Brubaker has played center on the class team for two years and has never been out-jumped by any man throughout a whole game.

Lafayette Franklin is a good forward but has difficulty in keeping up in the required number of subjects to play.

Earle Walker is a first year man but has plenty of speed to overcome his inexperience.

William Duston is a good man but has seldom been seen in action this year. He is a ruiner of records made by forwards.

Dale Winterbourne has appeared in only a few games. In these he has showed promise of being a good player.

Melchior Wilson is a first year man who is slow to overcome his [illegible]. He will be a good player when this is accomplished.

George Nelson is a new man and is slow in overcoming his inexperience.

SENIORS, V. H. S.--Top Row--Harold Worcester, Lowell Thomas, Emarine Jones, Homer Huffaker, Stephy Potochnick, Francis Needham, Will Dodsworth, Will Hayes.

Bottom Row--Ruth Emens, Electa Franklin, Edna Newman, Gertrude Lamb, Anna Bullock

Victor High School Class of 1909, featuring Lowell Thomas (second from left). MARK PERDEW

Victor. While in high school, Thomas also worked for one of the local newspapers, the *Victor Record*, where he gained invaluable experience he would use in his journalism career. He also wrote for *The Sylvanite*. The following is an example of his early work published in the April–May 1909 issue:

> *"Commencement! And Then What?"*
> *By Lowell J. Thomas, '09*
>
> *BOTH young and old of the present day cannot help realizing that we are now living in an age of gigantic problems, which present themselves to every man. The successful man of today must have an alert mind; whether or not it is well stocked it must be alert and ready to grasp and solve any new problem however difficult. The youth of yesterday, who are the men of today, are doing what their grandsires considered absolutely impossible. This, I think, is due to their superior collegiate training, and therefore young men and women of the Victor High School consider well before giving up a higher education.*
>
> *The persons who are always referring to the college man who comes home unable to hold any but a laborer's position seldom look upon the other side of the question. One writer says: "If the colleges were as careful of the quality as the quantity of their product these opinions could not be held."*
>
> *In reality there must be numerous evils connected with college life. We are told there are dangers "from soft culture courses," "college honors not being sought for," "the professors of the large institutions, we are informed, are inaccessible," "the students have an idea that they ought to see life, and thus neglect their college duties," "the desire for the diploma," and etc.*

At age eighty-nine, two weeks before he died, in the summer of 1981, Thomas paid his last visit to Victor High School and his old hometown. One of Thomas's teachers was Mabel Barbee Lee. She had also grown up in Victor and returned to teach in 1906. She always claimed that Lowell Thomas was her favorite student. Apparently he felt the same, as he mentioned her often in his broadcasts and even interviewed her in a live broadcast.

Throughout the years, the high school building underwent a variety of improvements and changes. According to Mark and Tarla Perdew, current owners of the school building, walls were added to create more rooms, the south fire escape was covered and then uncovered, and in 1939 the retaining walls and stairs from the Victor Avenue side were constructed to create the playground area in front of the school. Mark says that perhaps the most interesting and "bewildering" of the improvements was the construction of an outdoor swimming pool just south of the main structure. Apparently, the pool leaked when it was filled with water and was therefore never used. The area is now filled with mine tailings and used as a sand volleyball court.

Victor High School continued serving the educational needs of Victor through the ups and downs of the mining town until 1954, the last year the historic institution served as a high school. In 1955 the Victor and Cripple Creek schools were combined due to a drop in student enrollment, and classes were held in Cripple Creek High School for students in grades seven through twelve. Elementary students in grades one through six were taught in the old Victor High School. When the schools were consolidated, so were the sports teams. The Victor "Miners" and Cripple Creek "Pirates" became the "Pioneers."

Unfortunately, as the town's population continued to dwindle in the early 1970s, the Cripple Creek–Victor school board voted to close the Victor school and bus the students to Cripple Creek.

For the next few decades, the school building was used by a variety of businesses, including a return to teaching as a photography school owned and operated by Al and Suzie Weber for more than a decade. After 1987, the building was again used for various business ventures, including as apartments created out of converted classrooms that were rented out on a weekly and monthly basis. Then the school sat vacant for several years until the Webers reclaimed it in December 2003.

In January 2006, Mark and Tarla Perdew, directors of the Rocky Mountain Soccer Camp (RMSC) since 1992, purchased the old Victor High School building as a permanent home for the RMSC. Today the

Rocky Mountain Soccer Camp operates four-day live-in camps and three-day team camps out of the Elevation Training Center during the summer months. Renovation and upgrading of the old school building takes place throughout the other nine months of the year, which allows the historic building to now comfortably hold forty-eight campers along with staff in the facility. The Perdews have developed a small training area on the old schoolyard; they also utilize the Gold Bowl Athletic Field and Brian's Park Rink, which are owned by the City of Victor. Their motto is "Making history in the midst of history."

In this way, children once again roam the halls and attend classes in the classrooms and practice and play in the schoolyard at Victor High School, one of the great landmarks of Victor, "The City of Mines."

In 1923 the citizens of the mountain community of Conifer erected the **Conifer Junction Schoolhouse** (26591 Barkley Rd., Conifer). The one-story building was a fine example of the early twentieth-century American Movements architectural style. The most notable change in style was the entrance to the building. Heretofore, most school buildings had a single entry into the main building. The Conifer Junction

Victor High School (center, up on the hill) now serves as a soccer school. MARK PERDEW

Schoolhouse featured steps leading to the entry porch, where three doors offered entry to the building. Inside, the one-room school educated the area's students for more than thirty years. During this time, the school building also served as a community social center, where local events such as potlucks and social dances were held. The last school term was 1965. The building was converted to use as a preschool, which operated until 2012.

NOTES

1. Shaputis, *Where the Bodies Are*, 36.
2. Park County historian Christie Wright.
3. Archives of the South Park Heritage Association.
4. Dyer, *Echoes of Como, Colorado*, 76.
5. Park County historian Christie Wright.
6. Park County Office of Historic Preservation, Fairplay, Colorado.
7. Kaelin, *Pikes Peak Backcountry*, 145.
8. Celinda Reynolds Kaelin, past president, the Pikes Peak Heritage Society.

Chapter Eleven

The Michigan Creek School Murders

Park County is also home to the **Michigan Creek School,** the scene of a murder spree in the summer of 1894.

In 1875 Thomas M. Dunbar filed a preemption claim, located along the Tarryall Road. Following Dunbar's death in 1891, his sons, Charles and James, inherited the ranch. It was about this time that Charles

A newspaper drawing of the Michigan Creek School, where the murders occurred. PARK COUNTY HISTORICAL SOCIETY

Dunbar erected a one-room log cabin school on his property, which he named the Michigan Creek School.

In the summer of 1871, Benjamin Ratcliff, a Civil War veteran, and his new bride, the former Elizabeth McNair, arrived in Park County. Ratcliff filed on a homestead, where he established a cattle ranch. Ratcliff's land was adjacent to the Dunbar Ranch. While Ratcliff and Thomas Dunbar enjoyed an amicable relationship, Charles Dunbar and Ratcliff became adversaries.

Ratcliff was popular with several other ranchers in the area. He joined the local Rancher's Association and was quite active in local politics. It is worth noting that years later, in 1892, Ratcliff nominated Samuel Taylor to serve as county commissioner.[1]

Tragedy struck the Ratcliff family on October 13, 1882, when Elizabeth McNair Ratcliff and her fourth child died in childbirth. Now a widower, forty-one-year-old Benjamin Ratcliff struggled with running his cattle ranch and raising his three children. After two years, Ratcliff sent his daughters, seven-year-old Elizabeth and five-year-old Lavina, to his wife's sisters in Missouri. For the next several years, Ratcliff and his son, Howell, operated the Ratcliff cattle ranch. Sporadically, young Howell attended classes at the Michigan Creek School.

After ten years in Missouri, the Ratcliff girls, now teenagers, returned to their father's ranch. Seventeen-year-old Elizabeth had a severe limp due to lack of proper medical attention following a fall. Because of Elizabeth's disability, Ratcliff felt the seven-mile commute to the Michigan Creek School was too much for his daughter and a hardship on the family. In 1895 Ratcliff sent a letter to George Miller, superintendent of the Michigan Creek school board, with the following requests: (1) that the school be moved closer to the Ratcliff ranch; (2) that a homebound teacher be assigned to teach his children; and (3) that textbooks and materials be provided as they had been provided to other homebound students in the area. Ratcliff's requests were denied.[2]

Tension mounted between Ratcliff and the members of the Michigan Creek School Board. Nasty rumors regarding the Ratcliff girls were circulated throughout the community. President of the school board, Lincoln Fremont McCurdy, who had once worked for Ratcliff, may have been the source of the rumors, for McCurdy told the other members of the school board that Elizabeth Ratcliff was pregnant—and that her father was the impregnator.

The Ratcliff family had no idea that such awful rumors were being spread about them until Benjamin Ratcliff received a letter from Mrs. Susan Crockett informing him of the nasty allegations. Dated August 22, 1894, the letter read:

> *Mr. Ratcliff,*
>
> *My letter to you is on a painful subject but I will endeavor to be as direct & brief as possible, but first let me remind you that your daughters need you to love and protect them and so do nothing rash. Take a sensible & practical view of the situation and remember I place myself in the position of reporter simply because I think it is right you should know & were our positions reversed, I am doing to you simply as I would be done by. McCurdy—on Lee's ranch—made the statement before the board of directors that one of your daughters—I do not know which—was six months pregnant. Whether this originated with McCurdy or not, I do not know. I have heard that he said he heard it. This report is generally known but is not generally believed. I will refer you to a few persons that I know have heard it. Sam Lassell, Mrs. Borden, Mr. & Mrs. Sanborn, Mrs. Lapham and Mr. Crockett. I am truly the well wisher of your family and self.*
>
> *Mrs. M. Crockett*[3]

For a time, Ratcliff took Mrs. Crockett's advice and did nothing "rash." He did send a second letter to Superintendent Miller, again requesting textbooks for home use. When Ratcliff was denied a second time, he filed a formal letter of complaint with the Superintendent of Public Instruction in Denver. The complaint fell on deaf ears.

A frustrated Ratcliff, knowing his children needed to continue their education, decided to confront the school board and its president, Lincoln F. McCurdy, personally to demand a retraction and apology for the false rumor. The opportunity presented itself when Ratcliff learned the date of the next school board meeting. Ratcliff arrived at the Michigan

Creek schoolhouse early on the morning of May 6, 1895. He carried his 1873 Winchester rifle and two holstered Colt 1851 Navy Revolvers. When the board members took their seats, Ratcliff got right to the point. He demanded an apology regarding his daughter's honor or he would file a slander lawsuit. At this point, the schoolboard treasurer, George Douglas Wyatt, "Sprang onto the floor, cracked his fist; his knife blade was sticking up here (hand gesture) and swore no living man should bring him before [a] court on a charge like that."[4]

Ratcliff testified that he then fired a warning shot. He further testified as to what happened next:

> *Taylor waved his left hand, put his hand into his overalls and waved his left hand in an angry manner and he says, "now boys," and they came down at me at a rapid gait, and talking and hollering, you couldn't hear what they said.*

Samuel F. Taylor was the man Ratcliff had nominated for the school board years ago. According to eyewitness testimony, Taylor moved toward Ratcliff and Ratcliff fired. The bullet hit the fifty-six-year-old board secretary in the face. Taylor was dead before he hit the floor. At this point, it seems as though rage overtook Benjamin Ratcliff. Ratcliff's trial testimony described what happened next:

> *I immediately turned to McCurdy, who came in around the end of the seats and fired at him from the seat there. I thought I had missed the first shot and I pumped in another.*

Lincoln Fremont McCurdy, school board president who was believed to be the source of the nasty rumors regarding Ratcliff's daughter, was shot twice in the back. Ratcliff then turned his guns on thirty-five-year-old George Douglas Wyatt, who was also shot in the back.

After this last act of murder, Ratcliff exited the Michigan Creek schoolhouse and rode his horse to Fairplay, the seat of Park County, where he turned himself in to Deputy Sheriff James A. Link.

Meanwhile, pandemonium broke out at the schoolhouse, now the scene of multiple murders. Doctor Scott was summoned to the scene. He examined George D. Wyatt, the only immediate survivor. Realizing Wyatt was dying, the doctor injected morphine into his patient to ease the pain and gave him a shot of whiskey for comfort. Temporarily fortified, Wyatt was able to provide the authorities with his account of the events before he died. The statement was printed in the May 7, 1895, issue of the *Rocky Mountain News*:

> *I was shot by Benjamin Radcliff* [sic] *as was also Samuel Taylor and L. F. McCurdy. No one else was armed; no blows were struck before the shooting. Radcliff claimed that we, Taylor, McCurdy and myself, had slandered him and said he had an intrigue with his own daughter. No attempt was made by any of the parties to assault Radcliff. Five shots were fired. No conversation took place after the first shot was fired.*

George Douglas Wyatt died four hours later. The Michigan Creek schoolhouse was now the scene of a murder investigation. Doctor Scott laid out the bodies for postmortem examination while awaiting the arrival of the Park County coroner, Doctor Mayne, from Como. The coroner's inquest was held at nine o'clock that evening. The *Rocky Mountain News* printed the following report in the May 8, 1895, issue: "The [coroners] jury viewed the sickening sight last night, made more ghastly by the light of flickering candles."

Coroner Mayne was quoted in the article, stating, "We are not trying this case, we are here only to determine the cause of death."

By the following morning, word of the murders had spread throughout the county. Shock and outrage fueled talk of lynching. Again, the *Rocky Mountain News* reported on the activity in Park County. The front-page article appeared in the May 8, 1895, issue:

> *Those who came early in the day found stiff and cold bodies lying on the floor of the uncouth log school house. One surrounded by a pool of blood, another on a course* [sic] *mattress. Over another corpse was the*

> *swaying body of a woman, distracted by grief, and moaning piteously for one spark of life in the cold, staring eyes, while huddled in a corner, shuddering with a fear they could not understand, was a group of children who wondered between their sobs, whether the cold, bloody form was the father they had romped with and who yesterday kissed them good-bye.*
>
> *At noon, Park County coroner, Doctor Mayne, released the results of the coroner's inquest: "We find that L. F. McCurdy, Sam'l Taylor and G. D. Wyatt came to their deaths from gun shot wounds from a gun in the hands of Benjamin Radcliff* [sic] *& that the shooting was done with felonious intent."*[5]

The following day, May 9, the largest funeral procession ever in Park County was assembled for the burial of the three murdered men.[6]

Benjamin Ratcliff was charged with three counts of premeditated murder. A Buena Vista newspaper of May 8 reported: "A large guard has been placed around the jail and will resist any mob that might come down to lynch the prisoner. He is closely guarded and no one is allowed to see or speak with him. Every precaution is being taken by the authorities to prevent any trouble."

Because of the high tension in Park County, a change of venue was granted at the request of Ratcliff's defense team. Park County Sheriff Wilson transported Ratcliff to the Chaffee County Jail in Buena Vista. An editorial in the *Denver Evening Post* dated May 8 supported the move:

> *This is well. It is better that he should be legally punished. His punishment should be quick and the full limit of the law. The case is a good one on which to commence that severity and promptness of punishment which will serve as an effective warning against murder and make life and the happiness of families a little safer.*

Former circuit court judge Vinton Garrett Holliday represented Benjamin Ratcliff during his murder trial. On July 15, just ten weeks after the murders of the three school board members, the trial began in the Buena Vista Courthouse in Chaffee County. Judge Morton S. Bailey's first order was to try Ratcliff for all three murders in a single trial. The prosecuting attorney, George Hartenstein, spent two days presenting the state's evidence, eyewitness testimony, and the late George Wyatt's account of the murders.

Holliday based his defense strategy on his client's "fits of temporary insanity." Eleven witnesses testified on behalf of Ratcliff, including his son. On July 20, the jury returned a verdict of guilty of premeditated murder on all three counts. Judge Bailey pronounced the sentence as "death by hanging." The date was set for the following month, and Ratcliff was transported to the Colorado State Penitentiary at Cañon City.

Ratcliff's attorney requested and was granted five days to file a motion for a new trial. Holliday's request was based on the grounds that the jury was given erroneous instructions. Holliday won the appeal, and a second trial was held in January 1896. The result was the same: guilty of murder on all three counts. Subsequently, Holliday filed an appeal with the Colorado Supreme Court based on his original defense: that his client was temporarily insane. The state supreme court agreed to hear the appeal, and on September 18, Holliday presented his case. The attorney's motions were denied, and the lower court's decision was upheld.

The execution of Benjamin Ratcliff was set for the second week of February 1897. When Ratcliff received the news, he declared: "I have given up part of my life [when] wounded in Civil War service and will surrender the remainder of it in the good name of [my] family."[7]

A last-minute appeal for a stay of execution to Governor Albert McIntire was denied. On the morning of February 8, Benjamin Ratcliff was hanged at the Colorado State Penitentiary. A reporter for the *Rocky Mountain News* filed an article that appeared in the February 9, 1897, issue. It read in part:

> *Radcliff* [sic] *was pinioned, the black cap drawn over his head and the noose adjusted, and all present watched the dial that indicated when the weight was to fall. Radcliff's neck was broken by the twitch-up. Fifteen minutes afterward, the body was cut down and the attending physicians state that death was instantaneous.*

Benjamin Ratcliff's body lay in a prison coffin for two days before it was claimed by an unnamed family member. The murder of three school board members at the Michigan Creek schoolhouse is known as the "most brutal and unprovoked murders in Park County."[8]

The Michigan Creek School never reopened. A few years later, the log building burned to the ground. It was a fitting end to a sad chapter in Colorado school history.

Notes

1. *The Flume*, September 8, 1892. See also: Wright, *South Park Perils*, 82.
2. Van Dusen, *Benjamin Ratcliff*, 127–34.
3. Wright, *South Park Perils*, 84.
4. Transcript of the murder trial, *The People vs. Benjamin Ratcliff*. Chaffee County court records, Buena Vista, Colorado.
5. Ibid.
6. Barth, *Pioneers of the Colorado Parks*, 254.
7. Ibid.
8. Park County Office of Historic Preservation, Fairplay, Colorado. See also: Barth, *Pioneers of the Colorado Parks*, 254.

Chapter Twelve

Frontier Teacher Mabel Barbee Lee

Mabel Barbee Lee lived in the midst of Colorado's last great gold rush of the 1890s. After receiving a fine academic education, she returned to the gold rush hills to teach. And what a teacher she was, as her former students attested.

Mabel Barbee was born in Silver Reef, Utah, on April 11, 1884, the eldest child of Johnson and Kate (Kitty) Appleby Barbee. Her brother, William Johnson, was born in 1893; her younger sister, Nina, died in infancy in a drowning accident.

Mabel's father served four years in the Confederate Army during the Civil War. After the war, John Barbee, as he was known, made his way west, looking for a new beginning alongside thousands of others. At Silver Reef, Barbee staked a mining claim and had moderate success. However, by 1892 the mine had been played out and Barbee had no income.

Hearing the news of Bob Womack's enormous gold strike on the south side of Pikes Peak, Barbee packed up his family and headed for Cripple Creek, Colorado.

Mabel was eight years old when the family arrived in what would soon be dubbed the "Greatest Gold Camp on Earth." Arriving by stagecoach, the family settled in at the Continental Hotel on Myers Avenue. As buildings were scarce in the new mining camp, Barbee moved his family into a tent near the mine he was working on Beacon Hill.

The following spring, an outbreak of diphtheria spread through the mining camp, causing a delay in normal activity, including school attendance. The school term resumed after Christmas, and Mabel was finally able to socialize with children her own age. However, the one-room log schoolhouse did not impress the nine-year-old. Mabel later described the setting in her memoir, *Cripple Creek Days*:

> *The dirt floor and roof gave off a dark, mushroomy odor. Light filtered through a weather-stained window at one side. The fourteen pupils, ranging from six to sixteen, sat huddled on boxes and benches around a potbellied stove to keep warm while we studied; and often, when blizzards swirled across the mountains from Pikes Peak, the smoking chimney smothered the fire and the pupils had to be sent home.*

Mabel witnessed the great fire of 1896. The conflagration raged through the mining camp, the wood-frame businesses and houses a tinderbox. Mabel and her mother watched in stunned silence as their home was consumed by hungry flames. The following day, what was left of Cripple Creek smoldered among the ashes.

The townsfolk came together to help one another and care for the injured. Winfield Scott Stratton, Cripple Creek's first millionaire, sent a trainload of goods, supplies, and tents for the homeless. Although very grateful, Mabel and her family found themselves living in a tent once again. Cripple Creek's mayor, George Pierce, rallied his town's citizens to rebuild "bigger and better." In their coverage, the *Cripple Creek Morning Times* quoted the mayor:

> *It will take more than a destructive conflagration to crush a city that is founded on gold, for as everyone knows, gold is refined by fire!*

Most of the town was rebuilt in brick. Fine two- and three-story businesses lined both sides of Bennett Avenue, the town's main business district. Among the new homes was Mabel's. Her father, John, built it himself, and it took a couple of years to complete.

During this time Mabel attended school at the new Cripple Creek High School. It was a splendid two-story building built in all red brick. Mabel later recalled:

I was seventeen the summer of 1901, and had finished the third year [junior year]. It began to look as though my father's hopes of sending me away to study would never be realized.

Shortly thereafter, it seemed as if luck had finally turned in John Barbee's favor. In the summer of 1901, the *Cripple Creek Times* reported:

John Barbee who has found more ore on Beacon Hill than any other operator in camp has made a phenomenal find on the Columbia. On Monday an unexpected vein was encountered on the west side of the shaft. Samples run $720 to the ton and the ore resembles the high grade of Barbee's first Orizaba, the adjoining property.

It was by no means a rich strike such as that of W. S. Stratton, but Barbee could now afford a few fine extras for his family. One of those was a college education for his daughter. He had decided Colorado College in Colorado Springs would suit Mabel well, so he wrote them a letter. Mabel later recalled:

My father was disappointed to hear from Colorado College that a school diploma was required for admission. It was suggested that he send me to Cutler Academy, instead, which also provided residence for students.

Rather than finish her basic education in Cripple Creek, Mabel's father paid cash for a year's preparatory classes at Cutler Academy in Colorado Springs. Mabel must have been thrilled:

Our house was soon in a turmoil of activity getting me ready for the great adventure. Molly Letts was as excited as though I were her own daughter and she went along with Kitty and me in an orgy of clothes-buying. The two women seldom agreed on what was suitable or becoming for a girl of my age and they rarely consulted me. Molly seemed to confuse my going away to school with getting married and favored frippery that could do double duty as a wedding outfit. Kitty gave in to her insistence that I have a black satin corset "to show off that nice figure." It was Mollie, too, who persuaded her to let me wear my skirts floor-length, with even a short train on my best suit, a black mohair lined with sage green taffeta. It was Kittie's idea, however, to arrange for Mlle. Watchke to marcel my hair and do it up in a pompadour and puffs on top of my head. How much taller and more sophisticated it made me look! I stumbled and almost fell off the sidewalk trying to catch glimpses of myself in the barbershop mirrors and store windows along Bennett Avenue!

In the spring of 1902, Mabel was looking forward to finishing her school term and returning home for the summer. However, a typhoid fever epidemic was raging in the mining camp. Even her parents had left in an effort to avoid the sickness. When they returned in late August, a reporter with the *Cripple Creek Times* interviewed John Barbee:

"There isn't another mining camp in the West that would make me turn my back on Cripple Creek."

These were the words of John Barbee, recently returned from an extensive stay in southern Utah. He needs no introduction to the people of the District. His friends are legion. All mining men know what his record has been in discovering some of the richest ore bodies in camp. Words from him are worthy of note and should encourage other prospectors to rustle the hills.

Mabel graduated from Cutler Academy and enrolled in Colorado College in the fall of 1903. She was able to work odd jobs for "spending" money, as she called it.

The year passed quickly and left me with a feeling of accomplishment. I went to see my father before starting my summer job clerking in a candy store. I could hardly wait to tell him about all the excitement of the past weeks—the good times and many friends, of my improved grades and the tuition scholarship I received.

During her time at Colorado College, both of Mabel's parents died—her mother, Kittie, in 1904 from pneumonia; her father, John, in his sleep in 1905. Mabel managed to secure a second scholarship to finish her 1905 term. Griff Lewis, a friend of her father's, set up a donation fund at his Cripple Creek pharmacy to help pay for Mabel's final year of college. It wasn't until much later that Mabel learned that jars had been set in all the stores in Cripple Creek with signs that read "For John's Girl."

In the fall of 1906, Mabel accepted her first teaching assignment, at Victor High School. She would come back to the mining district she loved and to her roots, as she later wrote:

> *I was reasonably sure of getting an appointment in some small-town school when I had a degree. It came a few days before Commencement.*

Victor High School's beloved teacher, Mabel Barbee Lee, was barely older than her students in 1906. MARK PERDEW

I was to teach Spanish and History in the Victor High School and my salary would be $1080 a year. The notification was signed by Griff Lewis, president of the School Board of the Cripple Creek District.

Both eager and a bit nervous on that first day of her new teaching career, Mabel later mused:

It had been fourteen years since I entered the log cabin school in Cripple Creek's Old Town. I was a child then, in the fourth grade. It was a far cry from that dirt floor to the fine two-story Victor High School where I had come as a new teacher. The responsibility weighed heavily on my mind. The boys and girls in my classes, it struck me, were the smartest I had ever known. When I heard them come scuffling up the stairs into the room, I was seized by stage fright. One sophomore lad in particular loomed as a continuous challenge to my meager knowledge of modern history. He was quiet mannered and fine-looking, with dark wavy hair and serious eyes that seemed to see through my thin pretensions. He was a hard though silent taskmaster. Before long I was immersed in cramming my head with world history, fortifying myself against his unexpected questions.

The name of the brilliant student was Lowell Thomas.

In 1908 Mabel married Howard Lee, a mining engineer in the district. Shortly thereafter, their daughter, Barbara, was born. Sadly, the marriage lasted only ten years, when Howard succumbed to the great Spanish Influenza epidemic of 1918.

Mabel did not teach during those ten years and found herself in a financial predicament following her husband's death. She and her young daughter moved to Colorado Springs, where she became Dean of Women at her alma mater, Colorado College. It was a position she held until 1929.

In 1931 Mabel became administrator for the founder of Bennington College in Vermont. She followed this position by serving in the same capacity at Radcliffe College in Cambridge, Massachusetts; Harvard

Summer School; the University of California at Berkeley; and Whitman College in Walla Walla, Washington.

When she retired in 1951, Mabel felt the need to return to the Cripple Creek District.

> *Before I realized it, 1951 had brought me to another milepost. The time had come to say good-bye to the college campus, and the signs at the crossroads were indistinct. I was conscious only of a longing to go home, back to the house on Golden Avenue in Cripple Creek.*

At the urging of her former student Lowell Thomas, Mabel began writing about her life in the mining district. Thomas often talked about his childhood in the area, and by this time he had a successful radio career and was branching out to a new medium: television.

In 1958 Mabel published the first of two books about her life in the Cripple Creek Mining District, *Cripple Creek Days*. In the foreword, Lowell Thomas wrote:

> *There's only one first day of school that I can recall. That was one September when we were all surprised to find that we had a young and stunning redhead for a teacher, a girl who obviously was only a few years older than we were. None of us ever wanted to play hooky from her class, and playing hooky was a thing we all dreamed of and occasionally did. Beautiful Mabel Barbee was one of the few teachers who could always hold our attention. She had a gift for storytelling, and then we just liked to look at her.*

Historic Schools Listed by Region

The Eastern Plains

South of Interstate 70

Alta Vista School, State Register 6/9/1999, 5PW.42

Aroya Schoolhouse

Bent County High School, Las Animas Junior High School, and Las Animas Middle School, National Register 7/30/2010, 5BN.382

Crowley Consolidated High School, National Register 6/9/1999, 5CW.27

Crowley School, National Register 7/28/1999, 5CW.26

Eads School Gymnasium, National Register 8/20/2013, 13000607

Hartman School and Gymnasium, State Register 3/13/1996, 5PW.74

Holly Gymnasium, National Register 4/24/2007, 5PW.268

Huerfano County High School, State Register 9/14/2005; National Register 11/2/2005, 5HF.2183

Kim High School and Elementary School, State Register, 4/24/2007, 5LA.1815; National Register 8/1/2008, 5LA.1389

North La Junta School, National Register 6/25/1992, 5OT.276

Second Central School, State Register 6/12/1996, 5KC.135

Springfield Schoolhouse, National Register 10/5/1977, 5BA.313

St. Mary School, State Register 9/10/2003, 5HF.2162

Wild Horse School, State Register 12/11/1996, 5CH.122

Wiley Rock Schoolhouse, National Register of Historic Places 2/20/2004, 5PW.196

North of Interstate 70

Ault High School, State Register 12/8/1999, 5WL.2772

Brighton High School, State Register 5/14/1997, B489; National Register 1/23/1998, 5AM.580

Central Platoon School, State Register 11/5/2001, 5MR.470; National Register 11/5/2001, 5MR.764

Colorado State Teachers College (UNC), State Register 12/09/1998, 5WL.2883

Daniels School, National Register 7/6/2005, 5WL.3168

Eaton High School, National Register 9/11/1996, 5WL.890

Greeley Central High School, State Register 3/10/1999; National Register 4/16/1999, 5WL.2916

Greeley High School and Greeley Grade School, State Register 7/23/1981, 5WL.315

Greeley Junior High School, National Register 10/11/2003, 5WL.2572

Hoyt School, State Register 11/29/2007, 5MR.870

Knearl School, State Register 11/5/2001, 5MR.764; National Register 1/31/1997, 5MR.627

Lincoln School, National Register 4/27/2010, 5MR.892

Old Trail School, National Register 4/20/2004, 5MR.818

Ovid High School, State Register 8/9/2000, 5SW.78

Prospect Valley School, State Register 3/11/1998, 5WL.2562

The Front Range

Interstate 25 South

Bellvue School, National Register 10/11/2003, 5LR.792

Black Forest School, National Register 11/3/1992, 5EP.1753

Castle Rock School, National Register 9/20/1984, 5DA.342

Central High School (Pueblo), National Register 11/14/1979, 5PE.521

Cherry Creek Schoolhouse, National Register 3/8/1988, 5AH.213

Colorado School for the Deaf and Blind, State Register 3/11/1998, 5EP.2740

Colorado State University, National Register 6/15/1978, 5LR.472

Colorado Agricultural College (Laurel Hall), State Register 12/13/1995, 5LR.1964

Mechanical Arts Building, State Register 12/13/1995, 5LR.1965

Nutrition Research Laboratory, State Register 12/13/1995, 5LR.1963

Simon Guggenheim Hall, State Register 12/13/1995, 5LR.1962

Corona School (Dora Moore), State Register 6/19/1978, 5DV.185

Curtis School, National Register 6/25/1992, 5AH.459

Denver East High School, National Register 7/27/2006, 5DV.2091

Denver North Side High School, National Register 7/19/1992, 5DV.1097

Denver South Side High School, National Register 7/19/1992, 5DV.1112

Denver West High School, State Register 9/20/2002, 5DV.1985

Douglas County School

Doyle Schoolhouse, National Register 4/10/1980, 5PE.391

Edison School, National Register 6/19/1985, 5PE.4215

Emerson School, National Register 9/26/1997, 5DV.1495

Evans School, National Register 10/3/1980, 5DV.155

Fruitdale Grade School, National Register 3/20/2013, 5AM.2084

George W. Clayton Trust and College, National Register 5/02/2006, 5DV.310

Glen Grove School, National Register 11/5/1974, 5DA.214

Indian Park School, National Register 2/8/1978, 5DA.211

Laurel School, National Register 10/31/1980, 5LR.463

Littleton Log Cabin Schoolhouse, State Register 4/18/1998, 5AH.1430

Lone Tree School, State Register 3/8/1995, 5DA.344

Loretto Heights (Colorado Heights University), National Register 9/18/1974, 5DV.162

Lowell Elementary School, State Register 3/8/1995, 5EP.3958

Melvin School, National Register 1/5/1984, 5AH.164

Old Fort Collins High School

Pinewood School

Pleasant DeSpain School, National Register 8/30/1990, 5AM.442

Pleasant Valley School

Plummer School, State Register 9/11/1996, 5LR.778; National Register 4/29/1999, 5LR.778

Pueblo Central High School (Stone Schoolhouse), National Register 11/14/1979, 5PE.502

Sacred Heart School, State Register 3/8/2000, 5DV.997

Spring Valley School, National Register 12/18/1978, 5DA.219

Stove Prairie School, State Register 3/11/1998, 5LR.848

Union High School, State Register 1/14/2000, 5AM.67

University of Denver, State Register 5DV.174

Westlake School, State Register 11/9/1994, 5BF.1

Westminster University, National Register 8/10/1979, 5AM.67

The Rocky Mountains & Western Slope

North of Interstate 70

Buford School, State Register 2/24/2006, 5RB.4419

Bunce School, State Register 5BL.2632; National Register 1/29/2008, 5BL.10293

Coal Creek School, National Register 7/18/2014, 5RB.3575

Coalmont Schoolhouse, National Register 12/13/1995, 5JA.1264

Colorado School of Mines

Dillon Schoolhouse

Dumont School, State Register and National Register 3/1/1996, 5CC.654

Foidel Canyon School

Frisco Schoolhouse, National Register 9/15/1983, 5ST.253

Georgetown Public School, National Register and State Register 11/13/1966, 5CC.3

Gilpin County School, National Register 7/4/1961, 5GL.7

Hahns Peak Schoolhouse, National Register 2/15/1974, 5RT.72

Highland School, National Register 1218/1978, 5BL.364

Ladore School, National Register 2/24/1975, 5MF.1127

Lay Schoolhouse, State Register 9/27/2012; National Register 3/20/2013, 5MF.7384

Mesa Schoolhouse, National Register 11/1/2007, 5RT.2389

Montezuma Schoolhouse, National Register 1/9/2007, 5ST.1043

Mount St. Gertrude Academy, National Register 11/3/1994, 5BL.1471

Perry-Mansfield School and Camp, State Register 3/8/1995; National Register 7/14/1995, 5RT.976

Rio Blanco County High School, State Register 3/10/1993, 5RB.2667

Salina School, National Register 8/3/1989, 5BL.26736

Silver Plume School, National Register and National Historic Landmark 11/13/1966, 5CC.3

Thorn Lake Schoolhouse

Tolland School

University of Colorado

Ward School, National Register 8/3/1989, 5BL.2673

South of Interstate 70

Alma School, State Register 12/11/1996, 5PA.871

Battlement Mesa School, National Register 4/21/1983, 5GF.135

Canda School (Pine Grove School)

Chromo School, State Register 6/12/1996, 5AA.1907

Coates Creek Schoolhouse, National Register 2/3/1993, 5ME.6985

Como School, National Register 6/30/2000, 5PA.407

Conifer Junction Schoolhouse, National Register 2/10/2014, 5JF.5107

Crestone School, National Register 1/9/1986, 5SH.1014

Cripple Creek High School

Debs School, National Register 4/28/2005, 5HN.642

Durango High School, State Register 8/8/2001; National Register 10/20/2001, 5LP.3443

Fairplay School, State Register 12/9/1999, 5PA.58

Florissant School, National Register 10/1/1990, 5TL.305

Four Mile School (Fruitmere School), Fremont County Register 97300029

Fruita Elementary School, State Register 3/10/1993, 5ME.4600

Garden Park School, State Register 11/20/2008, 5FN.2192

Garo School

Gas Creek School

Hartsel School, Park County Historic Landmark, designated 2/13/2003

Jefferson Schoolhouse

Kesner Memorial Building, State Register 9/10/2003, 5CF.1507

Madison School, State Register 1/24/1996, 5FN.1233

Marble High School, National Register, 8/3/1989, 5GN.2041

Maysville School, National Register 4/29/1999, 5CF.333

Missouri Heights School, State Register 8/11/1999; National Register 9/23/1999, 5GF.2735

Morrison Schoolhouse, National Register 9/4/1974, 5JF.194

Mount Saint Scholastica, National Register 1/15/1998, 5FN.35.1

Mt. Pleasant School, National Register 5/3/2006, 5AL.89

Nathrop Schoolhouse

Pleasant Park School, State Register 6/12/1996, 5JF.972

Poncha Springs Schoolhouse, National Register 1/25/1990, 5CF.130

Rimrock School, State Register 8/9/2000; National Register 10/12/2000, 5GN.1410

Rock Schoolhouse, State Register, 9/8/2000

Saguache Elementary School, State Register 8/11/1993, 5SH.124

Saguache School & Jail Building, National Register 5/2/1975, 5SH.124

Shawnee School

Smiley Junior High School, National Register 11/27/2002, 5LP.1411.56

South Cañon High School, National Register 10/24/2005, 5FN.1564

Tarryall School, National Register 5/16/1985, 5PA.407

Valley View School, State Register 9/10/2003; National Register 10/12/2003, 5CF.1598

Victor High School (Victor Historic District), Historic Landmarks of Colorado, 7/3/1985, #85001463

Westcliffe School, National Register 7/27/1989, 5CR.29

Willows School, State Register 12/9/1992, 5CR.213

Bibliography

Archives and Primary Sources

Archdiocese of Colorado.

Archdiocese of Denver. History of Our Lady of Mt. Carmel.

Chaffe County Courthouse. Transcript of the murder trial, "*The People vs. Benjamin Ratcliff.*" Chaffee County court records, Buena Vista, Colorado.

Colorado History Center. "New Deal Resources on Colorado's Eastern Plains, National Park Service." Colorado History Center. "Pleasant Hill (Towner) School Bus Tragedy Intensive Research Plan," 2012. Colorado History Center. "Reverend T. A. Rankin's detailed diary." Directory of Religious Properties, Colorado Historical Society, 2010.

Colorado Preservation Inc.

Colorado State Register of Historic Properties.

Denver Public Library Western History Department. *History of Denver's Four Historic High Schools.*

El Paso County Court Records, Colorado Springs, Colorado.

First Church of Divine Science archives, Denver, Colorado.

Georgetown Heritage Center archives.

Park County Office of Historic Preservation, Fairplay, Colorado.

Playground Proceedings. National Recreation Association, 1907.

Rio Blanco County Historical Society.

Ross, Ariana. *North, South, East, West—Denver's Iconic Public High Schools.* September 9, 2016.

Summit County Historical Society.

Tread of Pioneers Museum archives, Steamboat Springs, Colorado.

University of Colorado archives, Mary Rippon collection.

University of Northern Colorado archives.

Zion Baptist Church archives, Denver, Colorado.

Additional Sources and Interviews

Christie Wright, Park County historian. South Park National Heritage Association Archives.

Colorado Reporter Herald, "Pleasant Valley Is Larimer County's Oldest School" by Ken Jessen.

Craig Press, Craig, Colorado.
Janet Clark, Rio Blanco County Historical Society, April 11 and 12, 2018.
Linda Jones, past president, the Gilpin County Historical Society.

Newspapers

The various newspapers accessed for this work are noted in the text along with the exact quotes.

Journals and Periodicals

Fogelberg, Ben. "Eaton High School." Weld County. *Colorado History NOW*, August 2001.

Spring, Agnes Wright. "Food Facts of 1859." *Colorado Magazine*, May 1945.

Books

Barth, Richard C. *Pioneers of the Colorado Parks.* Caxton Press, 1997.

Betz, Ava. *A Prowers County History.* Prowers County Historical Society, 1986.

Blair, Edward. *Leadville: Colorado's Magic City*. Pruett Publishing, 1980.

Brettell, Richard R. *Historic Denver.* Historic Denver, Inc., 1979.

Catlett, Sharon R. *Farmlands, Forts, and Country Life: The Story of Southwest Denver*. Big Earth Publishing, 2007.

Davis, William E. *Glory Colorado! A History of the University of Colorado, 1858–1963.* Pruett Press, 1965.

Dyer, Mary. *Echoes of Como, Colorado; 1879–1973*. Self-published, 1974.

Eberhart, Perry. *Ghosts of the Colorado Plains.* Swallow Press/Ohio University Press, 1986.

Feitz, Leland. *Alamosa!* Little London Press, 1976.

———. *Cripple Creek!* Little London Press, 1967.

Granruth, Alan. *A Guide to Downtown Central City, Colorado*. Self-published, 1989.

———. *Central City, Colorado 1859–1999.* Self-published, 1999.

Hansen, James E. *Democracy's College in the Centennial State: A History of Colorado State University.* Colorado State University, 1975.

Harner, Ariana, and Clark Secrest. *Children of the Storm. The True Story of the Pleasant Hill School Bus Tragedy.* Fulcrum Publishing, 2001.

History of Clear Creek, Boulder and Gilpin Counties. O. L. Baskin & Co. Originally published in 1880, reproduced in 1971.

Howlett, William J. *Life of Bishop Machebeuf.* Originally published in 1898, reprinted by Regis College, 1987.

Kaelin, Celinda Reynolds. *Pikes Peak Backcountry.* Caxton Press, 1999.

Lee, Mabel Barbee. *Cripple Creek Days.* University of Nebraska Press, 1958.

Leyendecker, Liston E. *The Griffith Family & the Founding of Georgetown*. University of Colorado Press, 2001.

Lopez-Tushar, Olibama. *The People of El Valle, Pueblo, CO.* El Escritorio Publishing Company, 1997.

Marr, Josephine Lowell. *Douglas County; A Historical Journey.* B & B Printers, 1983.
McQuarie, Robert J. *Littleton, Colorado.* Friends of Littleton Library, 1990.
Museum of Northwest Colorado. *Early Craig*. Arcadia Publishing, 2013.
Nelson, Jim. *Marble & Redstone: A Quick History.* Blue Chicken Publishing, 2000.
Noel, Thomas J. *Buildings of Colorado.* Oxford University Press, 1997.
———. *Colorado Catholicism*. University Press of Colorado, 1989.
———. *Denver Landmarks & Historic Districts.* University Press of Colorado, 1996.
Norman, Cathleen. *In and Around Old Colorado City: A Walking Tour*. Preservation Publishing, 2001.
Norman, Cathleen, and Linda Jones. *Up the Gulch*. Preservation Publishing, 2003.
Pettem, Silvia. *Separate Lives: The Story of Mary Rippon*. The Book Lode, 1999.
Smiley, Jerome C. *History of Denver.* Times Sun Publishing, 1901.
St. Vrain Valley Historical Association. *They Came to Stay*. 1971.
Scott, Bob. *Slade! The True Story of the Notorious Badman.* High Plains Press, 2004.
Segale, Sister Blandina. *At the End of the Santa Fe Trail.* Bruce Publishing Company, 1948.
Shikes, Robert H., MD. *Rocky Mountain Medicine*. Johnson Books, 1986.
Shaputis, June. *Where the Bodies Are*. Arkansas Valley Publishing, 1995.
Smith, Jeff. *Alias Soapy Smith*. Klondike Research, 2009.
Van Wyke, Millie. *The Town of South Denver*. Pruett Publishing, 1991.
Van Dusen, Laura King. *Benjamin Ratcliff: Park County Pioneer, Civil War Veteran, Triple Murderer.* History Press, 2013.
Varnell, Jeanne. *Women of Consequence: The Colorado Women's Hall of Fame*. Johnson Publishing, 1999.
Vervalin, Gene. *West Denver: The Story of an American High School.* EHV Publications, 1985.
Walters, Hildred, and Lorraine Young. *More Prairie Tales.* Self-published, 1976.
Wright, Christie. *South Park Perils*. Filter Press, 2013.
Williams, Lester L. *Cripple Creek Conflagrations: The Great Fires of 1896 That Burned Cripple Creek, Colorado.* Filter Press, 1994.
Wommack, Linda. *From the Grave: A Roadside Guide to Colorado's Pioneer Cemeteries.* Caldwell, ID: Caxton Press, 1998.
———. *Murder in the Mile City.* Caldwell, ID: Caxton Press, 2016.

Index

S

T

U

V

W

About the Author

A Colorado native, Linda Wommack is a Colorado historian and historical consultant. An award-winning writer, she has written eighteen books on Colorado history, including *Murder in the Mile High City; Colorado's Landmark Hotels; From the Grave: A Roadside Guide to Colorado's Pioneer Cemeteries; Our Ladies of the Tenderloin: Colorado's Legends in Lace; Colorado History for Kids; Colorado's Historic Mansions and Castles; Ann Bassett, Colorado's Cattle Queen; Haunted History of Cripple Creek and Teller County; Growing Up with the Wild Bunch*; and *Cripple Creek, Bob Womack and the Greatest Gold Camp on Earth.* She has also contributed to two anthologies concerning Western Americana.

Linda has been a contributing editor for *True West Magazine* since 1995 and has been a staff writer for *Wild West* magazine, contributing a monthly article since 2004. She has written for the *Tombstone Epitaph*, the nation's oldest continuously published newspaper, since 1993. Linda also writes for several publications throughout her state.

Linda's research has been used in several documentary accounts for the national Wild West History Association, historical treatises of the Sand Creek Massacre, and as critical historic aspects for the Lawman &

Outlaw Museum as well as the Heritage Center, both in Cripple Creek, Colorado.

Linda feeds her passion for history with activities in many local, state, and national preservation projects, participating in historical venues and speaking engagements, hosting tours, and is involved in historical reenactments across the state.

She is a member of both the state and national Cemetery Preservation Associations, the Gilpin County Historical Society, the national Wild West History Association, and is an honorary lifetime member of the Pikes Peak Heritage Society. As a member of Women Writing the West, Linda has organized quarterly meetings for Colorado members of WWW for the past ten years, served on the 2014 and 2020 WWW conference steering committees, and recently concluded her term as a board member. Linda is the chair for the Women Writing the West DOWNING Journalism Award.